REV. IKE'S SECRETS FOR HEALTH, JOY AND PROSPERITY – FOR YOU!

A Science of Living
Study Guide

by
Rev. Frederick Eikerenkoetter, Th.B., D.Sc.L., Ph.D.
(better known as Rev. Ike)

Table of Contents

Forward

Rev. Ike and his Ministry have gone from success to success, from glory to glory, and as they do, Rev. Ike enriches the lives of all those who come in contact with his teachings. The Bible says, "I have come that you might have life and that more abundantly." (St. John 10:10) Those who continue to believe and support the good work that Rev. Ike has done have found a positive way of life and are receiving more and more of the blessings of Health, Happiness, Love, Success and Prosperity.

Rev. Ike's Science of Living Ministry began with only a handful of faithful supporters. Rev. Ike taught these people how to get turned on to life. He showed them how to be, to do, and to have the good that they desire through the Presence and Power of God, Infinite Good, within everyone. As more and more people joined his Ministry, Rev. Ike became known as the man of God who teaches "Don't wait for pie in the sky by-and-by when you die ... Get your pie now, with ice cream on top!"

Rev. Ike became spiritual advisor to millions of people of all races and religions and even to those with no religion. He taught them that the Presence of God-in-you is your Unlimited Resource of Good. Rev. Ike attracted people from all walks of life — ordinary people, the rich, the poor, the famous, movie stars, political figures, sports champions — even priests and rabbis! People who hear Rev. Ike's message really get turned on to life.

As Rev. Ike and his Ministry continued to grow and expand, they reached and blessed more and more people. And more and more people are being turned on to life RIGHT NOW! More and more people are acknowledging the Presence and Power of God within them RIGHT NOW! More and more people are enjoying the good work that Rev. Ike Ministries is doing RIGHT NOW! Rev. Ike says, "The enjoyment of good increases and multiplies the good." Rev. Ike had faith and courage that those who are being helped by this Ministry will support this good work and will continue to be blessed for it.

Although Rev. Ike made his transition in July, 2009, his spirit is alive and well and his teachings continue to inspire millions through his dynamic YouTube videos (RevIkeLegacy channel). You can also connect with Rev. Ike on Facebook for more free videos, audios, written lessons, articles, affirmations and so much more!

You can also sign for our mailing list of free lessons and more at our website, www.ScienceOfLivingOnline.com.

How to Use
"Rev. Ike's Secrets For Health, Joy and Prosperity
– FOR YOU!"

N O T I C E !

This is NOT a book to "finish reading." Read it through,
over and over. Read any chapter anytime in any order.
Study it. Practice its instructions. Then "practice the
practicing." Study it every day, every week, privately and/or
in a group.

Right here in these pages there is a wonderful opportunity for
you. The Science of Living teaching is an opportunity for you to learn
the truth about yourself — the truth of who you are in God, and who
God is in you. The Science of Living teaches about the Presence
and Power of God within you and within each man. Through this
positive teaching, you can discover the power that is within you
and learn how to use this power to be what you want to be, to do
what you want to do and to have what you want to have. Study of
the teachings contained in this Study Guide can help you to begin
a new, more creative, more abundant life, right here and right now.

This Study Guide contains one study chapter for each week of
the year. These Study Guide teachings have eternal applicability.
They should not be limited to a specific day or week. If you feel
that you have thoroughly absorbed the ideas in a particular chapter
before the week is ended, feel free to progress at your own rate. But
do not forget to go back again and again to previous lessons.

Each chapter in the Study Guide is the development of a principle
from Rev. Ike's Science of Living teachings. There are six parts to
each chapter: a scriptural reference, a Science of Living principle,
development of this principle, quotes to remember, an affirmative
treatment and questions for review. Some chapters also include a
section entitled, "Things To Think On."

This book can help you to learn how to achieve the kind of life
that you want to have, but you must study it and practice these
teachings regularly. The Study Guide is not designed to be read

only once and then put away. Spiritual growth and development involve continual study and practice.

Individual Study

Set aside a special time each day for reading the Study Guide. We suggest reading before you go to sleep at night to give your subconscious mind the opportunity to absorb these positive ideas while you are asleep. After reading and studying the body of the chapter, read the Quotes to Remember. Study and work with the Review Questions and the exercises in Things To Think On when included. You may want to write down your answers to questions, and then return to the chapter to determine if you have answered them correctly.

Right before going to sleep, say the Affirmative Treatment out loud to yourself. This helps to reinforce these positive ideas in your subconscious mind, and causes you to clearly define yourself in positive terms. As you make your positive affirmations, use Rev. Ike's visualization technique — in your mind see yourself with the good you desire, and get full of the feeling of already having it!

When you wake up in the morning, reread the Affirmative Treatment and say it out loud again. Thinking positive, healthy thoughts about yourself will start your day out correctly and will bring positive experiences into your life. Continue to study and practice these teachings every day.

We suggest combining individual study with family study and discussion when possible. This develops personal spiritual growth, and also strengthens family ties.

Group Study

Forming study groups with friends and neighbors will help to reinforce the benefits of individual study. When one person has not been formally designated as class leader, students should take turns acting as leader at each class section. While the method of learning is up to the leader and students to decide, we suggest that the leaders encourage individual participation through oral reading and class discussion. After the body of the chapter has been read, we suggest reviewing the Scriptural Reference and Science of Living Principle, and discussing their meaning in light of what has been learned.

The sections containing Review Questions and Things To Think On are designed to stimulate the student to clearly and objectively examine his own thinking and to put newly discovered ideas into practice. The Quotes To Remember should be read, and the individual answers to the Review Questions should be discussed. After this section has been completed, the leader may want the entire group to read the Affirmative Treatment out loud. The Affirmative Treatment is written in the first person, to reinforce the positive ideas discussed in the chapter on an individual level. At this time the leader should review Rev. Ike's visualization technique, instructing the students to see and feel themselves with the good they desire. An optional addition to group study is the singing of appropriate songs.

Whether you form your own study groups, or study on an individual basis, let the positive thoughts and ideas in this book become a part of you. Work with the teachings in the Study Guide daily and practice them in faith. These teachings can help you to transform your way of thinking, and thereby transform your way of life.

We hope you will take full advantage of this opportunity to begin a new, more abundant life through Rev. Ike's Science of Living Study Guide. We hope you will take this opportunity to be what you want to be, to do what you want to do and to have what you want to have.

International Weekly Study

In order that people all over the world, people of all races, religions and ethnic backgrounds may use this Study Guide — with everyone studying the same chapters at the same time all over the world — we have organized the chapters according to the Sundays of the year.

If you wish to participate in this international weekly studying, begin reading the first chapter of this Study Guide during the week beginning the first Sunday of the year. On the week beginning the second Sunday of the year, read the second chapter and continue in this manner throughout the year.

EXCEPT for specific holidays and occasions... For holidays that fall on a Sunday, such as Easter, Mother's Day and Father's Day, read the special chapter during the week beginning with that Sunday. For other holidays, read the special chapter during the week beginning with the Sunday before the holiday. See the index for special group study recommendations.

ALWAYS return to the place in the Study Guide where you left off and continue your weekly study with the next chapter. By counting the Sundays in the year, you will be able to begin anytime and join in the international weekly study.

The following chapters are especially recommended for group study use for specific occasions.

For Valentine's Day, see Chapter 7.
For Easter, see Chapter 15.
For Mother's Day, see Chapter 19.
For Commencement Day, see Chapter 22.
For Father's Day, see Chapter 25.
For Independence Day, see Chapter 27.
For Labor Day, see Chapter 36.
For Thanksgiving, see Chapter 47.
For Christmas, see Chapter 51.
For the New Year, see Chapter 52.

IMPORTANT WARNING

Do NOT try to "convert" others to this teaching by arguing, disputing or "preaching on street corners." Convert your own thinking from negative to positive by quiet study and self-contemplation. Preach these "good tidings" to yourself. Cast forth the "good-spell" (Gospel) into your own mind and affairs. So demonstrate the Power of Good in your life, until people come to you voluntarily to find out what you use. I call this "Reverse Evangelism."

"Be you transformed by the renewing of your mind."
— Romans 12:2

Chapter 1

YOU ARE WHAT YOU FEED YOUR MIND

Dr. Frederick Eikerenkoetter

It is written, man shall not live by bread alone, but by every word that proceeds out of the mouth of God. St. Matthew 4:4

A SCIENCE OF LIVING PRINCIPLE

You will never get any further in life than the ideas in your mind. It is important to feed your mind only right ideas.

There's a story I like to tell of a hot dog vendor who sold very fine hot dogs by the side of the road. His business was booming, people loved his hot dogs, and they bought more and more. The man believed in his business and the need for someone to do what he was doing. This man was so busy advertising and selling his hot dogs and making lots of money that he didn't even have time to read the newspaper or listen to the radio. Consequently, he never heard a word about a predicted recession or the need to cut back to save the economy. As long as he continued to offer his delicious hot dogs, his customers bought them. He kept selling, and they kept buying.

Then one day his well-educated son TOLD him that an economic recession was coming. His son TOLD him that people wouldn't have enough money to buy his hot dogs. And the hot dog vendor BELIEVED this, so he quit advertising. He quit trying to sell his tasty hot dogs. He started ordering less. He even went so far as to take down the sign at his roadside stand. And sure enough, people stopped coming to him. People stopped buying his hot dogs, and he went broke. Then he thought to himself, "How smart my son is, predicting this."

_____

Everything in life comes from the ideas in your mind.

_____

This story gives us an idea of how powerful your mind is! If you start believing something, it will happen. It doesn't make any difference whether your thought is good or bad, it will come about if you think it will come about. Those of you who follow my teachings have heard me say this many times. But it is such an important principle that it bears repeating. *Everything in life comes from the ideas in your mind.* Everything! This is what Jesus meant when he said, *"According to your faith be it unto you."* (Matthew 9:29) According to your idea about yourself, according to the ideas in your mind, be it unto you.

In other words, the experiences in your outer world come from the inner world of your thought. So be careful what you think, and be careful what you say. Feed yourself, feed your mind, right ideas. Never feed anything to your mind that you don't want in your experience.

Make Right Ideas Your Daily Mental Diet

You have to feed your mind *only* good ideas. You can pray for prosperity all you want, but if you have the idea of poverty in your mind, you'll never prosper. You can pray for the healing of your body all you want, but if you have the idea of sickness in your mind, you'll never be healthy. That's why I tell you not to listen when other people tell you bad things. Don't let bad thoughts into your mind or they will happen in your life. That's why I advise people never to listen to the 11 o'clock news before they go to sleep. All that bad news will just creep into your mind and before you know it, you're in a real fix. Remember, thoughts are powerful! Thoughts are powerful food for your mind. And that's why you should only think GOOD thoughts. Think only positive thoughts.

Feed your mind healthy ideas, or the world will give you negative ideas which will manifest in your life.

Beware of Junk Food

Bad thoughts are like what some people call "junk food." Junk food is unhealthy. It has no nutritional value for your body. Bad thoughts are also unhealthy. They have no value for your mind, your body, your spirit, or your life. So don't waste your time on "junk food" thoughts. Think only GOOD thoughts. In other words, GOOD thoughts for a good experience of life.

You know the saying, "You are what you eat." Well, I'm telling you, *you are what you think!* What you feed your mind in the way of ideas is what you become. So you'd better make sure those thoughts and ideas are nourishing.

Read the Label

Being careful of what you say is like being careful of what you eat. Next time you get ready to eat something, read the label on the package or container it comes in. If the word POISON appeared on the label, you wouldn't eat it. That's the same reaction you should have to negative thoughts: Don't eat them! When you start to have a thought, read its contents. If it's got BAD stuff in it, don't consume any of it! Throw it away. Bad thoughts will just bring negative experiences into your life.

"May I Take Your Order, Please?"

When you decide what you want, begin feeding your mind pictures of it. You will be amazed at how fast it will come about. This is what my visualization technique is all about. Visualize clearly in your mind the good that you desire. See yourself being, doing, and having it. Accept it in your mind, and it will come into your life. As Flip Wilson says, "What you see is what you get."

Dinner is Served

One of the best ways to feed your mind is to think and to say, "I CAN." This is one of the most positive thoughts you can have."I CAN" are words of ACTION! And action, like everything else in life, begins with a thought, an idea, and a belief. The affirmation "I CAN" promises action. You can't say, "I CAN..." and just sit there and do nothing. It makes you want to jump up and start doing!

The world belongs to those who take action. Say you CAN do something and you WILL do something.

Open a CAN for Dinner

Now what follows "I CAN..." is extremely important. Whatever you add to I CAN will come about. So feed your mind positively. Feed your mind with all the sweetness of life, and it will be yours. Say I CAN... I CAN... I CAN...

THINGS TO THINK ON

We all have to go to the market to get food to feed our bodies, but where do we go to get food for our minds? The marketplace of life, of course. Buyers beware, however. Be careful which items you buy. There are ideas, thoughts, words and pictures everywhere we go. In the city and country, we see billboards. In the subways we read signs and advertisements. In books and magazines, there are lots of words and pictures. And of course we are always listening to what other people are saying.

There's a lot of both good and bad stuff in the marketplace of life. You have to be careful to let only the good stuff into your mind. The way to "sanctify" your mind from negative thoughts is: Fill your mind with good and it will automatically eject and reject the bad.

QUOTES TO REMEMBER

"I think, therefore I am."   ~ René Descartes

"As a man thinks, so is he."   ~ Proverbs 23:7

"The ancestor of every action is a thought."   ~Emerson

AFFIRMATIVE TREATMENT

Right here, right now, I will begin to feed my mind ONLY good thoughts.

I won't waste my mind's time on idle thoughts.

I will let only good thoughts into my mind because then only good things will happen to me.

I will let only good words come out of my mouth because what I say is what I get.

I CAN decide what I want.

I WILL decide what I want.

I will GET what I want.

Thank you, God-in-me!

REVIEW QUESTIONS

1. In the story about the hot dog vendor, was there really a recession?

2. Why do you think it is important to feed your mind only good thoughts?

3. Discuss the pros and cons of listening to the news.

4. What have YOU been feeding your own mind? What is the result?

5. How should we deal with the different kinds of ideas that confront us?

6. What are some of the ideas we should and should not "buy"?

7. What is meant by "sanctify" your mind from negative thoughts and how do you do it?

Chapter 2

DEFINE AND DECLARE

Dr. Frederick Eikerenkoetter

He is able to do exceedingly, abundantly above all that we ask or think, according to the power that works in us. Ephesians 3:20

A SCIENCE OF LIVING PRINCIPLE

If you say, "I am beholding God-in-me as my answer," that word goes forth to make the answer appear. If you want the answer, you have to behold the answer. You have to be aware of the answer. You have to speak the answer. When you do this, the answer will unfold.

I cannot repeat too often the fact that you have to be specific. You have to be definite with the Infinite. *The Infinite can only become definite when you become definite.* You have to define and declare the good you want before you get it. By "the Infinite" we mean the unlimited God. By means of man, unlimited God can be, do, and have ANYTHING. But it is a person's responsibility to choose and define exactly what the Infinite will be, do, and have through him.

The Elevator of Life

A few times, I have caught myself standing in an elevator with the door closed. Then all of a sudden, when it's about time for me to be at the floor that I wanted, I realize that I haven't gone anywhere. I discovered I hadn't gone anywhere because I had not pushed the button. I had not defined and declared where I wanted to go! What a great example I think that is!

You know, some people are the same way in the elevator of life. They are just standing there saying, "Now elevator of life, take me wherever you want to take me." If you just stand there and are not specific, if you do not push the button that you want, then other people's pushing will take you different places. And many times you'll find yourself where you don't want to be! This is such an important principle that I want you to affirm this to yourself:

"I must be definite with the Infinite."

Some religious people pray this way: "Now Lord, you just take me wherever you want me to go." And then they have the nerve to wonder why they are not getting anywhere in life. If you pray like that, you are just like somebody standing in an elevator who doesn't push the button, and you wonder how you got down in the basement. You have to decide where you want to go and push the right button!

If you don't push your own buttons in life, the world will push the buttons for you. You have to define in your own consciousness where you want to go in life. Don't let the world mind choose for you and push you around. Don't let other people choose for you.

Choose You This Day

There is one thing that the Infinite will not do for the individual. This is very important for you to remember. And let me tell you, you will never hear it in the average church. *The Infinite will not choose for the individual.* God is not going to choose for you. The Almighty is not going to choose for you. It is you who must choose. It is you who must define what you are going to be, to do, and to have in life.

You cannot ask the Infinite to choose for you whether you are going to have a Cadillac or an Oldsmobile. As I've said before, and I thought it was very effective, the Infinite is not going to say to you, "Go thou and buy an Oldsmobile." The Infinite is not going to say to you, "Go thou and buy a house in Beverly Hills." The Infinite has given to you the ability to choose what you want to be, what you want to do, and what you want to have. The Infinite God says to man, "Choose *you* this day…" (Joshua 24:15) The Infinite God also says to man, "Command *you* me." (Isaiah 45:11) God serves man, when man serves God with definite requests.

The Infinite Will Support You

Once you make a choice and believe in it, you will have an instant, constant supply of all that you need to back up your choice. Define what you want to be, what you want to do, and what you want to have, and the Infinite will back you up. The Infinite will support you. The Infinite will work with you. Not only will the Infinite work with you, but the Infinite will work through you to bring about whatever you define and declare.

We read in the Scriptures this verse: "He is able to do exceedingly, abundantly above all that we ask or think, according to the power that works in us." Decide, define, and declare the good you desire and the Infinite Power will back you up. The Infinite Mind will back you up. Make your choice. And believe that it will come about. The Infinite will back up your choice and give you all ideas necessary, all of the *modus operandi*, and bring you together with all of the right people for every right purpose.

You Have To Work With This Stuff

When I make that audacious claim, "You can't lose with the stuff I use!" it means that you must *use* this "stuff" that I teach you for it to work for you. You can't just sit there and look at it and expect it to work for you. You must use the techniques I teach you. This is another thing about religious people. Sometimes religious people are so lazy. They don't want to cooperate with the Almighty. They don't want to work with the Power that is within them. But God can only work for you through you. Remember, "I and my Father are one." (John 10:30)

God is not going to work with you unless you work with God. You have to define exactly what you want and then declare it positively.

The Presence and Power of God-in-you can do nothing until you define exactly where you want to go in life. Your car will not take you anywhere you want to go unless you get in there and turn the ignition and start the engine. The elevator of life will not take you anywhere you want to go unless you push the right button! You have to cooperate with the power that is in that automobile or in the elevator, or you get no positive results.

You Have To Do Something

People say to me time and time again, when something happens to them, "Oh no, Rev. Ike, don't tell me I thought this experience upon myself. I didn't think this up." And I tell them, "No, you did not think that up. *You didn't think anything!*"

If you do not consciously think positives for yourself, you are going to get negatives. You can't do *nothing*. You have to do *something* positive to start the good appearing. You have to do something positive; you have to define exactly what it is you want before the answer will unfold.

This is a principle you have to work with. That is why in my Success Ideas every month I deal in the areas of definite positives: health, happiness, love, success, prosperity, and money. I deal in the positives of life. And as you work with my teachings, you will learn to be definite with the Infinite. You will learn to define and declare exactly what you want to be, to do, and to have, and it will begin unfolding in your life.

QUOTES TO REMEMBER

"Command you me."   ~ Isaiah 45:11

"I must become definite with the Infinite."   ~ Rev. Ike

"Choose you this day..."   ~ Joshua 24:15

"God serves man when man serves God   ~ Rev Ike
with definite requests."

AFFIRMATIVE TREATMENT

I am defining and declaring God-in-me as my answer, right now.

I am defining and declaring God-in-me as my all, as my completeness.

I am defining and declaring God-in-me as my health and my happiness.

I am defining and declaring God-in-me as love.

The love of God in my heart brings me together with all of the right people for every right purpose.

I am defining and declaring God-in-me as my success and prosperity.

My life is running over with success, prosperity, and an abundance of money to enjoy and share.

Thank you, God-in-me!

REVIEW QUESTIONS

1. What is meant by "the Infinite"?

2. When does the Infinite become definite?

3. What is one thing that the Infinite will not do for the individual?

4. Discuss what happens once you make a choice and believe in it.

5. Why is it not good enough just to pray, "Lord make me what you want me to be, give me what you want me to have…" etc.?

6. How do God and man serve each other?

Chapter 3

THEY CAN'T TAKE THAT AWAY FROM YOU!

Dr. Frederick Eikerenkoetter

Lay not up for yourselves treasures upon earth, where moth and rust do corrupt, and where thieves break through and steal. But lay up for yourselves treasures in heaven, where neither moth nor rust do corrupt, and where thieves do not break through nor steal; For where your treasure is, there will your heart be also.
St. Matthew 6:19-21

A SCIENCE OF LIVING PRINCIPLE

Everything good comes from the Presence of God within you. You must give this Presence your attention and your allegiance. *God put something inside of us that will not let us down — His Presence!*

Divine Riches await all those who discover their true identity. The Bible says, "If I be lifted up, I will draw all men [manifestations] unto me." (St. John 12:32) That means, if you feel good about this Divinity that is within you, it will bring you together with everybody and everything, even all the money, that you need. Affirm the following to yourself:

"I am glad that I have this Divinity within me that nothing can take from me."

If I can get you to live with this feeling, with this realization, with this consciousness, with this awareness, you will be able to walk through the lion's den and the lions won't eat you. You will be able to walk through the fire and the fire won't burn you. You will be able to walk through the waters and the waters won't drown you. You will be able to say to yourself, *"I have something that nobody and nothing can take away from me!"*

Don't Forget Where Your Source Is

The Presence of God-in-you is your everlasting Source of all good. When you discover this Source of all good within your mind and being, all needful things shall be added unto you. You "shall not want." You can never be deprived of good.

When you know and practice the principles of Mind Science, you have the answer to life. And in the words of the song, "they can't take that away from you." To function happily and successfully in the world, one must know and feel that he has something that is not subject to the world. An old spiritual says it thus:

This joy that I have, the world didn't give it to me...
This peace that I have, the world didn't give it to me...
And the world can't take it away!

Your source cannot be in the world or of the world. You must know that "God-in-me is my everlasting Source of all good." If you think that people and things are your source, then people and things can cut you off. But if you know that God-in-you and only God-in-you is your Source of all good, then "they can't take that away from you." God-in-you may use many different people and things to *deliver* your good to you but no person or thing is your source.

Love and bless the people, the ways and means that God uses to deliver your good to you — but NEVER forget where your Source is. People and things come and go, but God-in-you is forever your unfailing Source of all good. "NO, they can't take that away from you!"

Do not believe that people and things are your source; know that only God-in-you is your Source. This is the meaning of "Lay not up treasures upon the earth… but lay up treasures in heaven…" (Matthew 6:19-20)

If You Can Feel Good About Yourself, You Can Do Anything

I want you to know that, as long as you have this Divine Something, or whatever you want to call it, you are rich. Because it will lead you, it will guide you, to be, to do, and to have the good that you desire. If you feel good about yourself, you can do anything.

You have a right to feel good about yourself because God is in you. Say to yourself, *"I have a right to feel good about myself because God is in me."*

Man Thinks Of Himself as a Son Of A Gun

Instead of thinking of himself as the son of God, man thinks of himself as a son of a gun. Too many religions have taught us that this is what we are. And I firmly believe that evangelists — and I used to have to count myself in on that — are to a great extent responsible for the negative spiritual self-image that people have. Because the more you call people sinners, the more they are going to sin. I know better now. We are all children of God.

What you say is what you get.

The more you call people devils, the more devil you are going to get out of them. I am saying this especially for some of you little ladies who just pray and pray for God to save your husbands. Then you get up off of your knees and shake your finger in his face and say, "You old devil, you, I'm praying for you." And you wonder why he doesn't change. It is because you are always telling him the devil is in him. And you are addressing yourself to the devil!

If you address yourself to the devil in anybody, you're going to get more devil out of that person. If you're not careful, you will catch hell from it. I find it amazing the way some of these good religious ladies pray. They say, "Lord, change my husband. Lord, stop him from drinking. Lord, stop him from running around. Lord, bring him out of that house on the corner." You are asking God to do all of that, and you are the one who drove him there with your big mouth! When he comes home to you, you call him a devil and a demon. And some of the things you call him, I can't repeat. But when he stops at "Caldonia's" house, she calls him "honey."

Appeal to the God, to the Good Within Each Person

When you address yourself to a negative concept, what are you doing? You are projecting the wrong self-awareness. You should appeal to the God, to the good, that is within each person that you deal with on any level and in any category. I quote from Flip Wilson just about every time I talk, because he preaches more gospel in one sentence than some of us preachers have preached in centuries. He says, "What you see is what you get." It is also true that "What you *say* is what you get." What you say about yourself is what you are going to get out of yourself. Each person that you call the devil, you are going to get the devil out of him.

Your Heavenly Treasure

This may shock some of you, but you don't have to die to experience heaven. When you find the heaven in you, then you will find this heavenly treasure, this spiritual treasure within you. Nobody will be able to take it from you. People can't break through and steal it.

The heavenly treasure, the Divine Something of man, may be described further as Divine Self-Awareness. It can further be described as correct self-knowledge.

This is your treasure, your heavenly treasure, that no one can take from you: The knowledge of who and what God is in you and who and what you are in God. When you have this knowledge, you are rich. Because you can take that knowledge and be what you want to be, do what you want to do, and have what you want to have!

You lay up treasures in heaven when you know, love, and trust God-in-you as your only Source. You lay up treasures upon earth when you falsely believe that anyone or anything in the world is your source.

QUOTES TO REMEMBER

"God put something inside of me that will not let me down." ~ Rev. Ike

"God-in-me, and only God-in-me, is my Source of all Good." ~ Rev. Ike

"Whatever kind of word thou speakest the like shalt thou hear." ~ Greek Proverb

"Appeal to the good, to the God, within each person." ~ Rev Ike

AFFIRMATIVE TREATMENT

I lift up the Divine Presence of God-in-me and I give this Presence my attention.

I feel good about this God-in-me.

I feel good about this Divinity-in-me.

This Presence of God-in-me leads and guides me in ways of health, happiness, love, success and prosperity.

REVIEW QUESTIONS

1. Discuss what it is that you have that can't be taken from you.

2. What is the meaning of "Laying up treasures upon earth," and "Laying up treasures in heaven"?

3. How should you feel toward the people and things that God uses to deliver your good to you? Who and what are some of these?

4. Why is it your right to feel good about yourself?

5. Why is it so important to know your true Source?

6. How can you appeal to the good within each person?

Chapter 4

CREATE YOUR OWN GARDEN OF EDEN

Dr. Frederick Eikerenkoetter

Whatsoever a man sows, that shall he also reap. Galatians 6:7

A SCIENCE OF LIVING PRINCIPLE

Only when you have a clear idea of what you want will you get it. Deciding what you want is the first step in creating it.

I received a letter, not long ago, from a very enthusiastic lady. She was about to open her very own flower shop called The Garden of Eden. Now I like to think that she calls it that because, like the other Garden of Eden, this is going to be a *perfect* experience for her. She has worked long and hard for this chance, and she isn't about to be "tempted" away from this opportunity. Maybe some of her friends even tried to discourage her from this business venture, but oh no! She has figured out what she wants and suddenly, it is a reality.

This particular lady wrote me that all this is possible because she has followed my teachings and specifically because she used my Money Book. She learned to think right about her possibilities, and she faithfully planted Money Seeds. And look what sprouted: Her own business!!!

The Garden of Eden Flower Shop owner gives my teachings a lot of credit for her success. But I didn't create her business. She did it herself. She BELIEVED in herself. She thought positive thoughts about herself and her dream business, and that dream became a reality. SHE CREATED HER OWN GARDEN OF EDEN!

Plant the Seeds of Self-Discovery

I want each of you to understand that you can create your own Garden of Eden. Because "Garden of Eden" is just a useful term for the positive things you want to achieve or acquire. *Your* Garden of Eden is whatever makes you Healthy, Happy, Loving, Successful, and Prosperous. Think about it right now. Are you visualizing successful and prosperous experiences? That's your Garden of Eden. Are you visualizing freedom from sickness? Then that's your Garden of Eden. Are you visualizing a big house or a new car? Then that's your idea of the Garden of Eden. YOUR Garden of Eden is whatever fixed idea you have in your mind. And it can be whatever *you* want it to be.

Your Garden of Eden is whatever positive things you want to achieve or acquire.

You can start your own Garden of Eden, but first you have to decide what you want in your garden. You have to figure what seeds to plant to make what you want grow. Then you have to plant those seeds and nurture them until they bloom into what you want. But this all starts with a decision — the decision to know yourself — the decision to know what you want to be, to do, and to have. As you travel the path of self-discovery, you will learn many things about yourself. And what you want out of life is one of them.

Build a Good Greenhouse

Now these seeds of self-discovery will grow and flourish in your own Garden of Eden if you take care of them. Nobody else is going to nurture your ideas for you. You've got to do it yourself.

One way to nurture or help these seeds grow is to give them a positive atmosphere. I like to think of it as a greenhouse for ideas.

To make sure the seeds in your greenhouse of REALITY grow, *write* down your ideas. When you write down what you want, you are focusing all your conscious mind-power on getting it. That is why I always tell you to write to me and tell me what you want. It helps you to focus your mind. The Bible says, "Where there is no vision, the people perish." (Proverbs 29:18)

When you have clearly in your mind the good that you want, when you trust in the Presence and Power of God within, your ideas will sprout into reality. And I guarantee it! Mind power is that powerful! You can't lose with the STUFF I Use!

"Where there is no vision, the people perish."

Big Green Money Trees

Let's get back to your Garden of Eden. Everybody's Garden of Eden should include plans for lots of money. To get Money Trees to grow, you have to plant the idea of money in your mind. How are you going to do that? Try this: Visualize yourself surrounded by money. Think money all the time. In your mind see and feel yourself using and enjoying more money than ever before. See your hands, pockets, and bank accounts *full* of money. Picture your purse or wallet full of money. You see, you have to have a mental picture of what you want in your mind all the time. Don't ever let it leave.

"Tall oaks from little acorns grow."

You know what happens when you don't water plants, don't you? They turn brown, shrivel up, and die. Don't let that happen to your Money Trees. You keep watering those Money Trees with GOOD ideas, and they'll grow big and tall before you know it.

I'm fond of that saying by David Everett, "Tall oaks from little acorns grow." Part of the reason I like it is that my name, Eikerenkoetter, means "acorn planter." And part of the reason is that this quotation means that no idea is too small if you believe in it and help it grow into something bigger. Don't let people discourage you. Don't let the world-mind discourage you. If you envision a big oak, you go right ahead and plant those tiny acorns. And if you want big Money Trees, you'd better plant money seeds.

No idea is too small if you believe in it.

Forbidden Fruit

There is only one kind of forbidden fruit. Negative ideas. Now you know how powerful your mind is, and if you start putting bad thoughts into your mind, then bad things will happen to you. Negative ideas are like rotten fruit. Throw them away. Because one bad thought, just like one bad apple, will spoil a whole barrel of good ideas.

So, be sure you keep only good ideas growing in your garden. Because those good ideas will grow into your Garden of Eden.

THINGS TO THINK ON

A garden is a wonderful place, full of sweet smells and nice colors. Life should be the same way. Think of all the good things that grow from ideas because someone takes action and plants the seeds of something he wants to grow. What are some things you want to grow in *your* garden of life?

QUOTES TO REMEMBER

"Tall oaks from little acorns grow."   ~ David Everett

"A man of words and not of deeds is like a   ~ Anonymous
garden full of weeds."

"Our bodies are our gardens... our wills are   ~William
gardeners."   Shakespeare,
                                              Othello I, iii, 324

"Who loves a garden still his Eden keeps,   ~ Amos Bronson
Perennial pleasures plants, and wholesome   Alcott
harvest reaps

AFFIRMATIVE TREATMENT

Right now, I will create my own Garden of Eden.

I must decide what I want to grow there.

No one else can decide for me.

I must decide.

Now, I must get the seeds or ideas of what I want firmly planted in my mind.

I am visualizing my Garden of Eden.

As I believe in what I want, it will come to pass. It cannot be otherwise.

Thank you, God-in-me!

REVIEW QUESTIONS

1. What is meant by "whatsoever a man sows that shall he also reap"?

2. How is a seed like an idea?

3. What happens when you visualize something?

4. Discuss how you will go about creating your own Garden of Eden.

5. What ideas are you planting in your mind?

Chapter 5

PROSPERITY PATH

Dr. Frederick Eikerenkoetter

The Lord is my shepherd, I shall not want. My cup runneth over.
Psalms 23:1-5

A SCIENCE OF LIVING PRINCIPLE

Make sure that your mind is at peace with money. For money comes to you through your mind. Everything comes to you through your very own mind.

You condition your mind for whatever you want by loving the good which you desire. And, yes, I'm going to say it point blank: "If you really want to have a good experience of money, you have to learn how to love money positively and correctly."

You Have to Love Positively and Correctly

I want to say this again, and I'm going to spend some time on it, because this is a touchy area. This is where religious people lose out with the money thing. You have to love the good which you desire positively and correctly. If you really want a balanced, successful relationship with money, you have to love money positively and correctly. Notice that in all of my affirmations about money, I'm always careful to say, *"I do not serve money. Money serves me."* That's the balance. That's the trick. Once you start serving money, that's where the evil comes in. As a matter of fact, once you start serving *anything*, that's where the evil comes in. But everything should be loved in its place. I was so glad to come upon this Irish proverb some time ago:

"Money swore an oath that nobody that did not love her should ever have her."

In Your Mind, Come to Peace with Money

I write Study Guide lessons to money-condition your mind, because you have to come to peace with money in order to have it. If you don't come to peace with money, you're going to have money troubles. If there is the slightest subconscious feeling that maybe money is dirty, maybe it is evil, maybe you shouldn't have much of it, money will know it and will oblige your attitude. Money will stay away from you.

A Child of the Infinite Cannot Have Lack

Religious people have such hang ups about money that in some religious orders, people take the vow of poverty. They say, "I'm poor for Christ's sake." How can a child of the Infinite have lack? If you have the right understanding with money, you should take the vow of wealth. "I swear I'm through with poverty." As they say on the street, "I swear to God I've had enough of poverty."

Keep Your Relationship with Money Balanced

Be sure you keep your relationship with money balanced. You must let money know point blank that you love it and that you understand what the relationship is. And you must get to that point where money loves you. That's when your mind is really money-conditioned. You must get to that point where money loves you and just won't stay away from you. Every time you look around, here comes more money. The more you use it, the more it comes. The more you enjoy it, the more it comes.

While driving to New York City the other day, I noticed that the bridge toll had gone up to fifty cents. When we first moved to United Church it was only a dime. When I saw that increase, my intellect started to grumble. Then I reminded the intellect, "You remember what Rev. Ike said, instead of grumbling about these prices, say, 'I give thanks for money to buy whatever I need.'" So I said, "I give thanks for this fifty cents to pay the toll."

Be sure to keep your relationship with money balanced.

Learn How to Enjoy Money

I want you to start learning how to enjoy your money, even in small ways. Whenever you use money, if it's to get on the bus or the subway, enjoy it. Enjoy the fact that you have that fifty cents or that seventy-five cents. Enjoy money — and not simply in big ways. Some of you say, "I'm just waiting until I get a whole lot of money, then I'm going to do this, that, and the other." Start right now enjoying your money in many little ways. If you buy yourself a five-cent piece of candy, make it your particular business to enjoy that candy. If you only have fifteen cents for a package of chewing gum, enjoy it. If you learn how to enjoy money, you establish a love affair with money, and then money will love you.

Accept the Idea of Prosperity

I don't care how hard you work, if you have the poverty idea in your mind, you are never going to get out of poverty. You will never have enough money to meet your needs. You must accept the idea of abundance. You must accept the idea of prosperity.

I like the way the Bible expresses overflowing abundance in the 23rd Psalm, the 5th verse. In that Psalm, David simply says, "My cup runs over." That tells me that people who serve God ought to have overflowing abundance.

Here is one thing I never could understand growing up in fundamental religion. We would always recite the 23rd Psalm and say, "The Lord is my shepherd, I shall not want." At the same time, we would say, "Money is evil." But let me ask you — why do you scrape and scratch so hard to get money if it's evil? Why do you get up so early and work so late? But I say that he who serves the Lord should have overflowing abundance. "My cup runs over." To me that means — and I transliterated it — "My life overflows with every kind of good." Say it to yourself: "My life overflows with every kind of good."

Ideas Make Millionaires

You are the manifestation of the ideas in your mind. The money that you have exactly matches the kind of ideas that you have in your mind. The condition that you are in exactly matches the kind of ideas that you entertain in your mind. Someone has said so beautifully, "Ideas make millionaires." That is true, and also multimillionaires. Ideas make multimillionaires.

You cannot be a millionaire if you do not have the correct relationship with money. I don't care how you pray. Now there are those people who, from a financial and material point of view, are actually millionaires and some even multimillionaires. But they don't enjoy their money, because they do not have a balanced relationship with money.

Money is to be used! Money is to be enjoyed! Money is to serve you! And a person's function in relation to money is to be the master of money. Say to yourself: "I am the master of money. I am the master of all things, because I am aware of my own self-mastery. Because I am master of myself, I master all things that concern me."

QUOTES TO REMEMBER

"If you could only love enough, you would be the most powerful person in the world."   ~ Emmet Fox

"Everything comes to you through your very own mind."   ~ Rev. Ike

"Money swore an oath that nobody that did   ~ Irish Proverb
not love her should ever have her."

AFFIRMATIVE TREATMENT

I now take time to make sure that my mind is at peace with money.

I control the money in my life.

Money does not control me, money serves me.

Money loves to serve me.

Money loves for me to enjoy it, and to use it for my good pur¬poses.

Money is good.

Money is wonderful.

I welcome more and more money into my life.

I think of money correctly, use it correctly, and enjoy it correctly.

Thank you, God-in-me, for money!

REVIEW QUESTIONS

1. What happens when you love the good that you desire?

2. What does it mean to love money "in balance"?

3. What does money trouble indicate?

4. How can you make money love you?

5. How can the "love of money" lead to evil?

6. Why is the "lack of money" evil?

Chapter 6

YOU DESERVE GOD'S GOODNESS

Dr. Frederick Eikerenkoetter

For I say unto you, that except your righteousness shall exceed the righteousness of the scribes and Pharisees, you shall in no case enter into the kingdom of heaven. Matthew 5:20

A SCIENCE OF LIVING PRINCIPLE

It is not enough in life to live morally and ethically. You must also have the proper self-awareness to enjoy the riches of the kingdom of Heaven.

Sometimes in preaching about Brother Job, the fundamentalist minister uses the subject, "Why Do The Righteous Suffer?" In other words, "Why do seemingly good people suffer?"

Brother Job's children were taken away, his health was taken away, and his wealth was taken away. Even his wife said to him, "You might as well curse God and die!" Why did all these things happen to Job, a righteous man? But I ask you, was Job righteous or religious? I want to go into this in this lesson because sometimes some of you good people remind me of Brother Job.

Can the Morally Straight Suffer?

I've said this before and it bears repeating here: *You can be morally straight and mentally crooked, and you will still suffer.* You can be morally and ethically straight and correct, but if you do not know how to positively relate to your emotions and the processes of your mind, you will suffer. And this is what happened to Job.

Job said, *"The thing I greatly feared has come upon me."* (Job 3:25) And that is exactly what got Job — "the thing." He didn't even know what "the thing" was. Just like some of you, you don't know why you feel so bad. But you go around afraid of what might happen; you go around with your feelings dragging in the dirt. Then you go to a psychiatrist for ten years and pay him umpteen thousand dollars and you still don't know why you feel so bad — and your psychiatrist doesn't either!

It is not enough in life to live morally and ethically straight. You must also have the correct self-awareness. You must know yourself.

You have to learn how to lift up your feelings yourself — to lift up your emotions. You have to learn to control your feelings and your emotions yourself. You have to learn to go inside yourself and develop a positive self-image.

Alcohol and Drugs Are Not Working Techniques

It was my pleasure to share my techniques with the psychiatrists at the Harvard Medical School Department of Psychiatry in Boston some years ago. I'll never forget that session. I had all of those big, important, expensive doctors of psychiatry right at my fingertips. They were casing me out, and I was casing them out. I have a number of friends who are psychiatrists, and it always feels like a game of cat and mouse when I'm around them, because I know they are casing me out. But when I started explaining the philosophy of this Ministry, the positive self-image psychology that we teach, they all sat up and listened. And it didn't cost them umpteen thousand dollars!

One of my friends, a psychiatrist, told me that at their last psychiatric convention, psychiatrists drank more liquor than any convention in the history of that hotel. I won't tell you what city and what hotel. But I will tell you emphatically that liquor and drugs are not techniques that work.

You should not have to depend upon alcohol or drugs or anything outside of you to give you a "high;" they won't get rid of "the thing." When you do depend upon these things to give you a "high," you haven't found the real thing yet. You can find the real thing through the Presence and Power of God within you. This is the highest high.

It Isn't Enough to Be Moral and Ethical

It isn't enough just to be a good person, to be moral and to be ethical. It isn't enough to consider yourself righteous OR religious. You must have a proper self-identity. You must believe that you deserve God's goodness.

Jesus said, *"Except your righteousness exceeds the righteousness of the scribes and Pharisees, you shall in no case enter into the kingdom of heaven."* (Matthew 5:20) This even answers the question that Job asked, "Why do the righteous suffer?" Because they don't believe that they deserve God's goodness. They ask for God's goodness in their prayers, but they don't believe they deserve it.

If you don't believe you deserve God's goodness, what do you believe then? Are you believing you deserve the opposite of good? If you are, maybe that is why you are getting it!

Nothing Can Come To You Unless You Draw It

Many times, things happen to good religious people and people who think they are righteous, and they don't understand why. They say, "Now why would this person do me out of this? Why do these 'things' happen to me?" If somebody is always doing you out of something, watch out. It means that somewhere in your subconscious psychology, there is some kind of negative belief. It could be the belief that you are not deserving. *Nothing can come to you unless you believe you deserve it, and nothing can go from you unless you believe you don't deserve it.*

You are not going to get anything that you don't really believe you deserve. And if you do appear to get something that you really don't think you deserve — you think it's too good for you — don't worry, it will slip away. Somebody else will come along and take it off your hands. So it is very important that you think you deserve the best.

You Are a Child Of God

Your belief about yourself should be based upon your knowledge of who and what you are in God, and who and what God is in you. Your belief about yourself must be based upon spiritual reality. You deserve the best because you are a child of God. Say to yourself, "I deserve the best because I am a child of God." And when you pray, believe this. Believe you deserve all of God's goodness. Don't just say empty words.

Affirm to yourself: I deserve the best because I am a child of God. I don't deserve the best because I'm better than anybody else. I deserve the best because I am God's child and I deserve all of God's goodness.

QUOTES TO REMEMBER

"We must move from the problem state of consciousness to the answer state of consciousness."   ~ Rev. Ike

"The two great movers of the human mind are the desire for good, and the fear of evil."   ~ Samuel Johnson

"Law is intelligence, whose natural function it is to command right conduct and forbid wrongdoing."   ~ Marcus Tullius Cicero

AFFIRMATIVE TREATMENT

I make it my business to think right, feel right and talk right.

I want only good for myself and everyone else.

Because I know that I am God's child, I know that I deserve the best.

I see myself as God sees me.

I see myself as a Divine expression of the God Presence within me.

These are the thoughts that I lift up in my consciousness and these thoughts help uplift me and everyone in my experience.

REVIEW QUESTIONS

1. What happens when we do not relate positively to the processes of our minds?

2. Why do some seemingly good, moral, ethical, religious people suffer?

3. What does it mean if someone is always doing you out of something?

4. Discuss the importance of self-awareness and self-discovery.

5. What was it that brought Job's trouble upon him?

Chapter 7

LOVERS ARE WINNERS

For Valentine's Day

Dr. Frederick Eikerenkoetter

He that loves not knows not God; for God is love. I John 4:3

A SCIENCE OF LIVING PRINCIPLE

God is love. The Presence of God-in-you is love. You must know this before you truly understand love and how to love.

A songwriter wrote a beautiful song which said, "Love Is A Many-Splendored Thing." However, many times when we hear people talking about love, they don't have the slightest idea what love means. When some people say, "I love you," they mean, "I want you to do as I think you ought to do, and if you don't do as I think you ought to do, then you don't love me." In this lesson I want to talk about love to give you a better understanding of what loving and love are all about.

You Are the Starting Point of Love

You must first learn to love yourself correctly. Perhaps you are asking, "Why, Rev. Ike, shouldn't we love God first, others second, and ourselves last?" As a matter of fact, the other day, someone came up with a slogan which said, "I'm third." He is a gentleman whom I admire very, very much, but I disagree with him. I am not third. When it comes to love, each of us is the starting point of love.

You cannot love others correctly until you first learn how to love yourself correctly. This is what you must understand. Even if you are relating to a God-in-the-sky, how are you going to love a God-in-the-sky before you love yourself? You are the starting point of love.

When it comes to love, each of us is the starting point of love.

In Mind Science, we are always dealing with the subconscious mind. We are seeking to impress these positive ideas upon our subconscious minds. When we talk to ourselves, the subconscious mind sits up and says, "Oh, he's about to tell me something; she's about to tell me something. I had better listen." So once again I'm going to be purposely redundant and have you say to yourself, "I am the starting point of love."

How's Your Love Life?

Love must start with you. You cannot love or be loved correctly until you love yourself correctly. Your love life is the result of the way you love yourself. Your relationship with others is the result of the way you relate to yourself.

You cannot love others correctly until you first learn how to love yourself correctly.

On the sociological level we go around telling people, "Look, you should love one another." That's fine, but it doesn't begin there. This is why no kind of social panacea has been able to work yet. Loving one another begins with loving your individual self.

We have to get back to the individual and teach the individual how to relate to himself correctly and positively, because the individual is the first unit of society. This is why I love that beautiful song that says, "Let there be peace on earth, but let it begin with me." Here again, you are the starting point of everything in your life.

If you want to love and be loved, you are the starting point. You can't find love out there in the world until you first find love inside yourself. You can't give love unless, first of all, you love yourself and give this love out of your own correct self-understanding.

Feel Good About Yourself

I would like to take a moment to define the kind of self-love that I'm talking about. That type of love that I'm talking about is positive self-love. Positive self-love is not an ego trip, and that is important. Because, right away, if you don't understand this, you will say, "Well, Rev. Ike is on an ego trip and he's teaching people to go on an ego trip." But it's not that way at all.

Self-love may be described in a number of different ways. Self-love is positive self-esteem. Self-esteem is self-love. Another term for self-love is self-value. Self-love is really what you think about yourself. It's what you feel about yourself. Loving yourself correctly means that you feel good about yourself. You value yourself. You appreciate yourself.

Self-love is positive self-esteem.

Love the Good You Want

Whatever you love, you magnify and objectify. If you love the God-in-you, you become God in action. Say to yourself: *"As I love the God-in-me, I become God in action."* Whatever good you want in your life, love it. Love it as a part of you. Love the good in you and you will express and experience more good Whenever you do something good, just love it. Give thanks for it. Give praise for it.

When you dress yourself up so that you look good and smell good, stand in front of the mirror and look at yourself and tell yourself how good you look. Before I left for the office this morning, I stood in front of a full-length mirror, and I said these words, "God, you sure look good in me." The next time you stand in front of a mirror, say the words, "God, you sure look good in me."

43

Believe That You Deserve

Love yourself so that you believe that you deserve everything good. Away with this old religious notion, "Lord, you know I don't deserve it." Some people pray and say, "Lord, give me this, give me that. Now Lord, I know I don't deserve it." Well, if you think that way, you can forget getting anything.

The next time you stand in front of a mirror, say the words, "God, you sure look good in me!"

In life, you only get what you subconsciously believe you deserve. If you get kicked in the behind, you subconsciously believe that you deserve it. You men and women who have a spouse who treats you like a dog, it's because you don't love yourself correctly. You don't esteem yourself correctly. If your boss is down on you, it is because you are down on yourself. If you find that generally people are down on you, it's because you're down on yourself and you don't love yourself correctly. And that is the gospel according to Rev. Ike.

In life, you only get what you subconsciously believe you deserve.

Other People Treat Me Like I Treat Myself

You cannot really be mistreated unless somewhere in your life, somewhere in your mind, somehow or other, you mistreat yourself. I want to say this again. The things that people do to themselves on the psychological level, on the subconscious level, when they come back to them on the objective level, they don't recognize them. I want you to say this to yourself, *"Other people treat me like I treat myself."*

Are You Winning With Your Self-Image?

Unfortunately in much of the organized religious sector today, we have been taught to depreciate ourselves. For example, there is an old hymn that says, "For such a worm as I." That is a very blatant example of self-depreciation. Because if you think of yourself as a worm in the dust, you will experience what a worm experiences. What happens to a worm? A worm gets stepped on. A worm gets smashed.

If you are finding yourself getting stepped on in the game of life, it is because your self-esteem, your self-appreciation, your self-image, is not correct. You do not love yourself correctly. You do not value yourself correctly. You see, self-love is self-respect. If you value yourself correctly, if you esteem yourself correctly, if you feel right about yourself, then people are not always going to be stepping on you. All the world will respond to you as a winner in the game of life.

QUOTES TO REMEMBER

"When it comes to love, I am the starting point of love. I cannot love others correctly until I, first of all, learn to love myself correctly."

~ Rev. Ike

"Your relationship with others is the result of the way you relate to yourself."

~ Rev. Ike

"The more closely you associate yourself with the good, the better."

~ Plautus

"Love conquers all things ..."

~ Virgil

AFFIRMATIVE TREATMENT

I see myself loving and being loved in Divine order.

I love myself correctly.

I love the good in me.

I love the God-in-me.

Because I love myself correctly, I love others correctly and others love me correctly.

The love of God in my heart brings me together with all of the right people for every right purpose of love and business.

Thank you, God-in-me, for love!

REVIEW QUESTIONS

1. Where does love begin? Why?

2. What is the difference between positive self-love and an "ego trip"?

3. Your relationship with others is the result of what?

4. How do you love yourself correctly?

5. What happens to whatever you love?

Chapter 8

IT'S NOT YOUR SKIN, IT'S YOUR MIND

Dr. Frederick Eikerenkoetter

The Lord is no respecter of persons. Acts 10:34

And be not conformed to this world: But be you transformed by the renewing of your mind, that you may prove what is that good, and acceptable, and perfect, will of God. Romans 12:2

A SCIENCE OF LIVING PRINCIPLE

Your consciousness determines your experience. When you know your spiritual identity, you don't think of yourself in terms of race. The law of life and the law of the cosmos react to everyone on the same basis.

It would alarm some of you if you really knew what I was saying to myself when you tell me all of these things like, "Oh, Rev. Ike, I'm so sick. I've got arthritis, I've got this, I've got that…." Do you know what I say to myself when people tell me things like that? I say, "I don't believe it. There is not a word of truth to it." What I am doing is denying the existence of anything negative in your life. This is one of the techniques used to program life as we want it to be. To put it more directly, you must flatly reject what you don't want. You don't have to experience what you don't want.

Flatly reject what you don't want in your life.

Mental Laziness

What I'm teaching you is so simple. But you'd be surprised how few people do it. You see, the masses of people are spiritually and mentally lazy. They are too lazy to think for themselves. They will listen to the radio, to TV, to the news, and they will think whatever the media tell them to think. The media program them. The newscasts program them.

If you are too spiritually and mentally lazy to learn how to think for yourself, the world will do it for you. And before you know it, you will be in a hell of a fix!

Think It Down

Some people say to me, "Rev. Ike, don't tell me that I've thought this up on me. No, I didn't think this up." I say to them, "No, you may not have thought it up. You may not have thought it up, but did you think it down?" You see, what you experience in life depends on what ideas you accept and reject. You may not consciously accept an idea, but if you don't consciously reject it, that idea will manifest in your experience.

You don't have to consciously think sickness and disease to have them. You don't have to do that. The world has already cooked up a nice juicy pot of diseases for you. If you are black, you are supposed to have sickle cell anemia. Sometimes the black leaders will say to me, "Rev. Ike, what are you doing for sickle cell anemia?" I say, "Not a damn thing. I want no part of it. I will not have it. I do not want it. I'm not interested in it. I flatly reject the idea of it."

Have Some "Potage"

Back in the country where I was born, when kids grew up, they already had their diseases lined up for them — measles, mumps, whooping cough. People thought that you were DUE to have these things. If you didn't, you were some kind of a queer. You don't have to think negative things up. But you'd better think them down. All of these diseases are in the world mind, so you don't have to think them up. But if you leave a vacuum in your mind, if you do not flatly reject the idea of them, the world will give you some of its mess of "potage."

You may not consciously accept a negative idea, but if you don't consciously reject it, that idea will manifest in your experience.

Be Not Conformed to This World

Self-discovery is not just for the white folks or the yellow folks or the black folks. Self-discovery is for everyone who is willing to take the time and make the effort. Self-discovery is for everyone who has in his mind a concept for a better life — an idea of a better way to live — an idea of having and enjoying more.

"God is no respecter of persons" means that "as a man thinks so is he" regardless of race, creed or color. The Lord (Law of Mind) responds to every person the same. As Jesus said, "According to your faith, be it unto you." (Matthew 9:29) Your faith is what you believe about yourself. Believe the best about yourself and that's what you bring into your life. Believe the worst about yourself and that's what you bring into your life. It's not your color. It's your mind.

You can pull yourself up by your bootstraps to be something, to do something, and to have something. We are all individualizations of God. I like to put it this way:

People of different races are God wrapped in different color packages.

I want you to think about what Brother Paul tells us: "Be not conformed to this world, but be you transformed by the renewing of your mind." (Romans 12:2) And it doesn't matter about your race or your present station in life. Your destiny depends on how you program your mind, how you program your consciousness.

QUOTES TO REMEMBER

"Your consciousness determines your experience." ~ Rev. Ike

"There is no expedient to which a man will not go to avoid the real labor of thinking." ~ Thomas Alva Edison

"Thinking is the hardest work there is, which is the probable reason why so few engage in it." ~ Henry Ford

"People of different races are God wrapped in different color packages." ~ Rev. Ike

"Color is of the mind." ~ Hon. W.D. Muhammad

AFFIRMATIVE TREATMENT

Right here and right now, I reject all negative appearances in my life.

God-in-me is my everything, and I don't have to worry about anything.

This is the truth of me.

I program my life for all the good that I desire.

God-in-me is my health.

I reject all appearances of disease.

This healthy thought about myself keeps me full of vim, vigor, and vitality, from birthday to birthday.

I program my life for success and prosperity.

Knowing that my destiny depends upon how I program my mind, I consciously program my mind for Health, Happiness, Love, Success, Prosperity, and Money.

I program my mind for all of the Good that God is.

Thank you, God-in-me.

REVIEW QUESTIONS

1. What should you do with an idea or a suggestion you don't want?

2. What is mental laziness?

3. What does your destiny depend on?

4. What does it mean to program your mind?

5. What programs your mind if you don't?

6. Can a bad thing happen without a person "thinking it up"? How?

7. Does the Lord (Law of Mind) respond to people of different races in different ways?

Chapter 9

DECISIONS, DECISIONS, DECISIONS...

Dr. Frederick Eikerenkoetter

What do you want me to do for you? (words of Jesus to a blind beggar)

Thou shalt also decree a thing and it shall be established unto you. Job 22:28

Whatever things you desire, when you pray, believe that you will receive them, and you will have them. Mark 11:24

A SCIENCE OF LIVING PRINCIPLE

The God within you has ways of bringing about that which you decide you want. But you must make the decision of exactly what it is you want.

How many of you have heard the expressions, "Well, that's the way the mop flops!" Or "That's the way the cookie crumbles!" These are two common expressions of frustration many people use when they have lost control of their circumstances and things happen to them that they don't like. But today we're going to put an end to all that. You are no longer going to be subject to the fickle finger of fate, lady luck, or the devil next door. In this lesson, you are going to learn how to take control of your life by making the right decisions.

You can make things happen as you want them to happen when you learn to make positive decisions.

One of the most important things in life is learning how to make decisions. And yet there is no formal training to teach you how to do this. No amount of formal education will equip you in this area of your life.

Be Specific, Be Clear

There are four basic steps to good decision making. Let's go through them one at a time.

❶ DECIDE EXACTLY WHAT YOU WANT

YOU be sure you know exactly what it is you want.

Here are some questions you can ask yourself to help you determine what you want: Do I want more friends? Do I want better relationships with the people around me? Am I happy with the way I live? Do I want a bigger or better home? Do I want more money to meet my needs? Do I want good health? Do I want to be less dependent on others? Do I want a better job? Ask yourself questions like these, which will help you focus on exactly what you want in your life. Now, take the time to write down the answers.

❷ DEFINE THE ANSWER

Look at how you answered the questions. Whatever the answer, decide it and affirm it. If you want to have more money in your life, decide it. Affirm to yourself, "I decide that I'm going to have more money in my life!"

Now look deep down in your heart. Can you recall early dreams that you left behind because they seemed impossible? Can you recall other people talking you out of the good desires of your heart? Don't hold back. *Decide what it is that you want. Decide what it is you want to be. Decide what it is you want to do. Decide what it is you want to have.* Say to yourself: "I decide to be happy," "I decide to be healthy," "I decide to love and be loved," "I decide to be successful and prosperous."

❸ BELIEVE IN THE ANSWER

The third step is a step in faith. Believe God-in-you will fulfill your desires. Know that God is Unlimited, Infinite Good. Know that God is everything, and that God is on your side. As someone once said, "If God is for you, who can be against you?" The Presence and Power of God within will bring your decision to manifestation. This is really what faith is all about. Faith means that you understand the Law of Mind. A decision made by the conscious mind will be brought about by the God within. Jesus said, *"Whatever things you desire, when you pray, believe that you will receive them, and you will have them."* (Mark 11:24)

❹ DON'T ASK HOW

This fourth step looks easy, but it can be tricky. Rest and relax in the knowledge that the answer will come about. Don't ask how. In the first book of the Bible, the Lord decided that He wanted light. And once He decided, what did He do? He said, "Let there be light." And what followed? Light. He did not scratch His head and say, "Oh, I wonder how I can make some light." He didn't say, "Oh, how can I make the world, it's such a big job."

Once you decide what you want and announce the decision, the "how" will take care of itself. When the Divine Mind said, "Let there be light," light came from everywhere. Light balled itself up into fire and began to shine like the sun by day and like the moon by night.

The God within has ways of bringing about that which you decide upon. Sometimes it is something that the conscious mind can't even accept as a possibility. The Bible says, *"His ways are beyond finding out."* (Romans 11:33)

If you believe, you will be led, and motivated by God-in-you to take the right action. You will be connected with the right people, ways, and means. Cooperate with God.

Miracles for You!

You read in my Action Magazine all the time how so-called miracles come about because people use my teachings, because they have faith that God within will provide. If you follow these four steps properly and with faith, those things which seem like miracles will happen in YOUR life! God within finds ways to create things that seem like miracles. And when you know how to make decisions, when you have a clear idea of what you want to be, what you want to do, and what you want to have, the God within will work for you. You will be able to create your own miracles.

QUOTES TO REMEMBER

"The great decisions of human life have as a rule, far more to do with the instincts and other mysterious unconscious factors than with conscious will and well-meaning reasonableness."

~ Carl Gustav Jung

"Decision has power. The moment you make a decision, everything necessary for the fulfillment of your decision begins to happen."

~ Rev. Ike

"Indecision is the second root of all evil!"

~ Raymond Charles Barker

"Jesus, on the main line, tell Him what you want."

~ Hymn

"Once a decision was made, I did not worry about it afterwards."

~ Harry S. Truman

AFFIRMATIVE TREATMENT

Right here and right now I decide clearly in my mind what I want to be, what I want to do, and what I want to have.

I hereby decide that I want more health, more happiness, more love, more success, more prosperity, and more money!

I am not going to get hung up on how it will come about.

I know that God within is working in my favor to bring these good things into my life.

Thank you, Father!

Thank you, God-in-me!

REVIEW QUESTIONS

1. What is the best way to take control of your life?

2. Why is it important to make decisions?

3. Once you make a decision, what happens?

4. What does it mean to "co-operate with God"?

Chapter 10

THE THRILL OF IT ALL

Dr. Frederick Eikerenkoetter

My word that goes forth out of my mouth shall not return unto me void, but it shall accomplish that which I please, and it shall prosper in the thing whereto I sent it. Isaiah 55:11

And the Lord answered me, and said, Write the vision, and make it plain… Habakkuk 2:2

A SCIENCE OF LIVING PRINCIPLE

When you speak in faith, when you speak in love, when you speak in the spirit, the words you speak become the word of God that goes forth out of your mouth to accomplish that which you have spoken.

We are told in the Scriptures, *"Write the vision, and make it plain."* This means that you should know exactly what you want and be very clear about it.

If you speak your word, and it is definite and positive, what you want will come to you. And it will come to you in ways which might seem miraculous. Now everything may not come in a seemingly miraculous way, and I want to be very clear on this. If you learn how to be definite and positive in describing the good which you desire, and in speaking your word concerning it, it will have to come to you. And that is what I find so thrilling about this teaching and about this

Ministry. Every day I get so many letters from people who have put my teachings into practice. They write and tell me of the many ways their good desires come about.

Sometimes I have experiences that really blow my mind, too. Recently, I had one such experience. But I have to warn you that sometimes these things sound crazy. You see the intellect really can't handle more than it can explain by reason. But this is the truth. This is what happened to me.

The Story of the Blue Shoes

I wanted some dark blue shoes, so I decided to go down to Hollywood Boulevard in Los Angeles. I went to a particular shoe store, and I spoke to the manager whom I know. I said, "I want a pair of blue shoes. I don't want any high heels or high platforms." As I looked around, the only blue ones I saw had very high heels. And I was afraid I might fall off of those! I told him I wanted regular heels and soles. He had quite a conversation with his salesman to establish whether or not they had those blue shoes, and then they turned to me and said, "We don't have any of them."

The manager went back to helping another gentleman that he was waiting on before I came into the store. Then inside of one minute he went into the stockroom and brought out a pair of blue shoes for the other gentleman. (Watch this now. You don't have to believe it because my intellect doesn't either.) I said to him, "How is it that you told me you didn't have any blue shoes like I wanted? Those you have there are blue shoes." He looked at the shoes he had in his hand and said, "I never saw those shoes before." I said, "Bring them over here." He brought them over and guess what? They were exactly my size. He called the clerk over, and they both swore they never saw those shoes before. And they walk in and out of that stockroom at least a hundred times a day.

The more you become aware of the power of your mind, the power of your word, the more you will demonstrate it.

There are several things about this incident which really astounded me. Number one, the manager picked up those shoes within one minute after I asked for them and just after he got through explaining he didn't have them. Both the salesman and the manager established that they didn't have them. Number two, they were exactly my size, and exactly what I wanted. In the third place, they did not know what to charge me for the shoes, because they had *never* seen them before. They had to *make* a price! I had made the shoes with my word! So I bought them. All that is too much to be a coincidence.

Here is another thing. They went back to where they found those shoes and found some more. And so I said to him, "You send me my commission for the rest of those shoes, because I spoke them into existence!"

The More You Are Aware, the More You Will Demonstrate

This is not the first time this kind of thing has happened to me. It happens to me all the time. It happens to me because I know the Infinite mind power of God-in-me, and because I keep my conscious mind as well as my subconscious mind tuned in to the good I desire. You don't have to believe that if you don't want to, but I find these things happening in my life more and more. I want you to realize that you have the same power. *The more you become aware of the power of your mind, the power of your word, the more you will demonstrate it.*

Be Choosy

Now I want you to notice what I did to get those shoes. I defined exactly what I wanted. That is my "word." Your word should always define exactly what you want. Many times when you speak your word, you don't get what you want because you don't say exactly what you want. When I go into a store now, and I did it purposely on the occasion of the shoes, I purposely do not say "Do you have such-and-such?" I say, "Give me such-and-such," or, "I want such-and-such." When I went in for those shoes, I didn't say to them, "Do you have ...?" I said, "I want. Give me." They said they didn't have them, but I didn't accept that. What did I say? "Give me. I want." And I defined exactly what I wanted. I have told you this many times before:

Be choosy. Know what you want. Say what you want. When you speak, be very definite.

When I went in there and said exactly what I wanted concerning those blue shoes, I was very definite. And those blue shoes had to come from somewhere.

Now, some people speak their word negatively by always talking or always complaining about things that they don't like. And here again, you know what a complaint is? It is a negative word that brings you more to complain about. Once you become a chronic, habitual complainer, you are always speaking more into existence to complain about.

The Thrill of It All

Your mind power will do anything for you that you make clear. Now what could be more thrilling than that? We're told in the Scriptures, *"Write the vision, and make it plain."* Many of you keep your subconscious mind completely confused. Your mind doesn't know what you want. And you don't either.

You are always speaking your world of experience into existence. And it's up to you to speak it as you wish it to be. But first of all you have to know what you want to be, to do, and to have. Everything that you want, be definite about it. And you'll surprise your intellectual process at the results you begin to get when you learn to say exactly what you want. Oh, the power in your word.

QUOTES TO REMEMBER

"Your mind power will do for you anything   ~ Rev. Ike
that you make clear."

"What I cannot be sure of, I cannot truly want." ~ Sir Isaiah Berlin

"The more you become aware of the power of your mind, the power of your word, the more you will demonstrate it." ~ Rev. Ike

AFFIRMATIVE TREATMENT

I now enter the secret closet of my mind, and I look upon the stage of my imagination.

I see myself being what I want to be, doing what I want to do, and having what I want to have.

I see myself as a healthy person.

I see and feel the health and strength of God flowing in my soul, mind and body.

I see myself as a happy person.

I take happiness wherever I go and I spread joy wherever I go.

I see myself loving and being loved in Divine Order.

I see myself as a successful, prosperous person.

I see myself having lots and lots of money.

I have money but money does not have me.

I see green all around me.

Thank you, God-in-me.

REVIEW QUESTIONS

1. What happens when you speak your word definitely and positively?

2. When you become more aware of your mind power, what do you do?

3. What should your word always do?

4. What have you been speaking into your life?

Chapter 11

FROM POSSIBILITY PATH TO REALITY ROAD

Dr. Frederick Eikerenkoetter

With God all things are possible. Mark 10:27

All things are possible to him who believes. Mark 9:23

A SCIENCE OF LIVING PRINCIPLE

When you believe in the Presence of God within you, you be¬come God in action.

"With God all things are possible," is a fantastic statement. However, this wonderful realization is a BLANK TICKET, and will get you nowhere unless you FILL IT IN with faith, by deciding and affirming EXACTLY WHAT you want. All things REMAIN possibilities until you define what you want, and by faith make reality out of possibility.

It is not enough to believe that "all things are possible." You must decide WHAT you want and by faith and action make it a reality.

Do not stop at believing that good health is possible. Decide that you shall have it, and it will become a reality. Do not stop at believing that happiness is possible. Decide that you shall have it, and it will become a reality. Do not stop at believing that love is possible. Decide that you shall have it, and it will become a reality. Do not stop at believing that success is possible. Decide that you shall have it, and it will become a reality. Do not stop at believing that prosperity is possible. Decide that you shall have it, and it will become a reality.

Possibilities are NO GOOD until they are made into reality by faith and action. *"Where there is no vision, people perish,"* (Proverbs 29:18) with UNBORN POSSIBILITIES. Unlimited possibilities are seeking birth through the mind of man.

Jesus said, *"All things are possible to him who believes."* (Mark 9:23) I want you to notice something in the above verses of Scripture because there is something between the lines here. Let me tell you what I read between the lines. Noticing that "With God all things are possible" and that "All things are possible to him who believes, I get this: The person who believes is God in action. Affirm this to yourself: "When I believe, I am God in action."

_____

Your oneness with the Infinite is your basis of power.

_____

The greatest delusion of mankind is that he thinks he is separate from God. That's the only sin there is. Because once man believes that he is separate and apart from God, once man believes that he is not the son of God, then he acts like a "son of a gun." Every other sin comes from this delusion. So if one believes in his oneness with God, all things are possible to him.

God does not know you as something apart. The Infinite does not know you as someone apart from itself. Say that to yourself and focus your whole mind on it. Say it this way: "The Infinite does not know me as someone apart from itself. God believes in me." And you see, when you, as an individual expression of the Infinite, believe in the Infinite and the Infinite believes in you, there is a connection of faith and power that is UNSTOPPABLE. Say to yourself: "I believe in God; God believes in me. I AM unstoppable!"

You're Off and Running

This belief is the starting point of making reality out of possibility. This is knowing the basis of your power. Your oneness with the Infinite is your basis of power. And Jesus, the individual, kept telling us of his identity with the Infinite Father. During all the miracles that He performed, while He did His good work, He kept saying, "This is my Father working through me. The Father that dwells within does the work." And when you believe in the Presence of God within you, you become God in action. When you believe in the goodness of God within you, when you believe in the mind of God, the intelligence of God within you, you become God in action. "In all your ways acknowledge Him, and He will direct your path."

Through the Door and Up the Path

You know, if you believe in yourself and you set forth with positive thought and positive action, the doors of opportunity will swing open for you. Doors close in people's faces because of their attitudes more than anything else. And when doors open, they open because of their *attitudes*.

So you have to develop the proper attitude. Accept the possibility of the good which you desire. Affirm this to yourself: "I accept the possibility of the good which I desire."

An interesting thing happens once you accept an idea. Once you accept an idea in your mind, and you open your mind to these right ideas, an inflow of other correlating ideas begins to take place. Everything you need will begin to come to you, but you must first accept the possibility in your mind.

Accept the possibility of the good which you desire.

One Step at a Time

First of all, in making reality out of possibility, open your mind to the possibility of good. After you do that, see the good already established, perfect and complete, with the eye of your mind. Then you will be connected by God-in-you to the right people, and your faith will compel the right ways and means and propel you to right action.

Check Your Map

I always get letters from people who are not only making reality out of possibility, but in some cases are practically making impossibilities happen. One such letter was from a young man in the south. He had been writing me for two years concerning the life sentence that he was serving in prison. He wrote to tell me that the impossible had come to pass. The judge had ordered him discharged. He is home free, discharged from a life sentence! You see, when you believe in the possibility of good, when you believe in the power of God within you, you can make even the impossible possible.

Avoid Dead-End Roads

Why is it that people always find it so easy and so simple to believe in the possibility of evil, rather than the possibility of good? I keep thinking about the young lady I spoke to when I walked down the aisle at my Church. She said to me, "Rev. Ike, I wrote to you and asked you to pray for me to get a job. And Rev. Ike, I got that job this week." And immediately she started crying and said, "Now Rev. Ike, I want you to pray for me that I don't lose my job." She had just received a blessing, but right away began thinking about the possibility of losing it. Watch that.

THINGS TO THINK ON

I want you to think for a moment about the three things that you desire the most and write them down. Say to yourself, "What are the three things that I desire the most?" And if you can't stop at just three things, keep listing the good you desire. Make the list as long as you want.

Believe in the possibility of these things, and you will become God in action. God will begin to act in you and through you and as you, to bring about the materialization of that good which you desire.

QUOTES TO REMEMBER

"All things are possible to him who believes."   ~ Mark 9:23

"If you believe in yourself, and set forth with positive thought, and positive action, the doors of opportunity will have to swing open to you." "As a man thinks, so is he."   ~ Rev. Ike

AFFIRMATIVE TREATMENT

I open my mind.

I open my mind to great and happy possibilities.

I open my mind and make a decision about the good I want.

I visualize what I want.

I see myself being, doing, and having the good I want. Thereby, I make reality out of possibility.

REVIEW QUESTIONS

1. Why is it not good enough to believe that "all things are possible"?

2. What does decision have to do with making reality out of possibility?

3. Read "between the lines" of the two Bible verses at the beginning of this lesson. What is the revelation?

4. What happens when people believe in the possibility of evil rather than the possibility of good?

5. What are "unborn possibilities"?

6. What is the one sin that brings about every other form of sin?

Chapter 12

ROOT FOR YOURSELF

Dr. Frederick Eikerenkoetter

Be you transformed by the renewing of your mind. Romans 12:2

I press toward the mark for the prize of the high calling of God. Philippians 3:14

A SCIENCE OF LIVING PRINCIPLE

You only get what you give to yourself. You give to yourself by believing in the best for yourself and of yourself. You give to yourself by believing that you deserve the best, then the best will come to you from within you.

You should be your biggest fan. I know to some people this may sound like egotism, because you have been taught, for the most part in fundamental religion, to depreciate yourself and to say, "Well, I don't deserve anything." Some of you have even been taught to pray like that fellow in the Bible, *"Lord, I am not even worthy of the least of thy mercies."* (Genesis 32:10) But I say to you that you should be your biggest fan. *You should root for yourself.* I advise you to get in front of the mirror every day and say good things about yourself, to yourself.

Self-Motivation Means Self-Encouragement

You should encourage yourself. Self-motivation means self-encouragement. This is so important, because I've seen a lot of people sit around on the sidelines of life, discouraged, disgusted, busted, depressed, suppressed, and unpressed. But you have to learn how to encourage yourself.

You should be your biggest fan. You should root for yourself, encourage yourself.

A young man said to me some time ago when he was In a disgusted, busted condition, "Rev. Ike, I'm just waiting for somebody to give me a push." If you sit around on the sidelines of life waiting for somebody to come along and give you a push, more than likely you will be trampled under the feet of those who are marching on to victory. You have to learn to encourage yourself.

Play to Win

Come with me for a moment into the arena of sports, particularly scholastic sports. I remember back in high school, we always made it a point to have a lot of pretty girls sitting along the sidelines to root for the team as it played. And many times, I have seen a losing team come out of its losing streak and win again because the players' friends and associates on the sidelines began to root for them.

If you don't believe you can be a winner, then no one else will either. Believe in yourself, and others will believe in you.

That's why I say to you, learn to root for yourself. Learn to cheer yourself on. How dare you sit around on the sidelines of life disgusted and discouraged, looking for somebody else to come along and encourage you, when you don't even encourage yourself!

I am going to give you this little technique that some people may think is egotism, and I want you to use it. I want you to start using it immediately. But don't let people who don't understand what you are doing see you do this. They will think that you have lost your senses. That is the trouble with some people, they have too much sense. By that I mean some people know every reason why they can't be, why they can't do, and why they can't have. They talk themselves down and talk themselves out of their good desires.

Impress Yourself First

I want you to get in front of your mirror and talk to yourself. But before you do, make yourself look good so that you will enjoy looking at yourself. I want you to write this on your heart: *The first person that you need to impress, that you need to make a favorable impression on, is yourself.*

Always remember that. When you make a favorable impression upon yourself, you will project that favorable impression upon everyone you come in contact with.

Make a Good Impression

I want you to try this technique. Impress yourself favorably before you go out to do whatever you are going to do. Groom yourself until you look extra good to yourself. Bathe yourself expertly and sprinkle on a little extra cologne or perfume to enhance your natural sweetness, until you smell good. Then look yourself straight in the eye in that mirror and root for yourself. Say to yourself, "Oh boy, I am going to be a big winner today. I have got it in me to succeed." Remember, you are talking to yourself. Stand in front of that mirror and tell yourself, "I see God-in-me. I see good in me. I see the talents of God-in-me."

The first person that you need to impress, that you need to make a favorable impression on, is you.

Every day, before you go out to face the day, stand in front of the mirror and root for yourself. Even without a mirror, you can affirm good things about yourself. You can root for yourself.

Build a Successful Self-Image in Your Mind

What you need to do first is to build an image in your mind of the person that you wish to be. And constantly, throughout the day, in your mind, see yourself being, doing, and having the good which you desire. And keep on encouraging yourself. Say good things to yourself and about yourself. This is self-motivation. Keep telling yourself that you are going to make it. Say to yourself, "I am going to make it!" Can you feel that God-Power in you? Rooting for yourself like that stirs up the God-Power within you. It motivates you onward.

You are in the biggest game of all. You are in the game of life. You don't want to tie in this game, you want to WIN. And in order to WIN, you have to motivate yourself. Remember and affirm to yourself: "I AM A WINNER!"

QUOTES TO REMEMBER

"The first person that you need to make a favorable impression on is yourself." ~ Rev. Ike

"People do not lack strength, they lack will." ~ Victor Hugo

"You should be your biggest fan. You should root for yourself." ~ Rev. Ike

"Ah no, 'twas not the chance you lacked! As usual — you failed to act!" ~ Herbert Kaufman

AFFIRMATIVE TREATMENT

I am going to be a winner today and every day.

I am in this game of life to be a winner, and I am going to win!

I am not going to tie.

I am going to march on to victory.

I see myself as a winner and I root for myself.

WOW! I impress myself correctly. And I impress others correctly.

I AM a winner!

Thank you, Father.

Thank you, God-in me!

REVIEW QUESTIONS

1. Explain how it happens that you only get what you give to yourself.

2. Discuss the meaning of these terms: "root," "fan," "tie," and "egotism."

3. Why is rooting for yourself not egotism?

4. Discuss why you should root for yourself.

5. Why is it important to impress yourself?

6. What is the best way to make a favorable impression on yourself?

7. Why should you not let certain people see and hear you rooting for yourself?

Chapter 13

SON OF GOD
OR "SON OF A GUN"?

Dr. Frederick Eikerenkoetter

For God so loved the world, that He gave His only begotten son, that whosoever believes in Him should not perish, but have everlasting life. John 3:16

A SCIENCE OF LIVING PRINCIPLE

Wherever you go, go with thanksgiving in your heart. Go with a smile on your lips and know that you are a child of God.

In this lesson I want to discuss something that is very important, something that is going to help you in every way. I refer to the words of the Scriptural passage above, "For God so loved the world, that He gave His only begotten son."

First of all, the Christian theologians, in particular, interpret this text to mean that Jesus was God's only relative. But I take issue with them. If Jesus was God's only child, what does that make the rest of us? Ask yourself, "Am I a son of God or a 'son of a gun'?"

Divine Sonship

To me, this text indicates that God so loved everyone that He gave *everyone* Divine Sonship. The only begotten Son of God is the one relationship which each person has with God. And whoever believes in his Divine Sonship shall not perish, but will enjoy everlasting life. I transliterate "everlasting life" to mean "the livingness of God."

Here is another Science of Living transliteration of John 3:16: "God so loved *everyone*, that He gave each person Divine Sonship. And whosoever believes in his own God-given Divine Sonship will not suffer in the human sense of self — but will enjoy the livingness of God."

The only begotten son of God is the Divine Sonship of each person. Divine Sonship is the one relationship which each person has with God. When you believe in your Divine Sonship, when you believe that you are a child of God, when you know it, in the words of the Gospel, you will have "everlasting life" — the livingness of God.

"I and My Father Are One"

It was not Jesus' purpose to say to us, "Hey, look at me. I am the Son of God! I am God's only child! God never had a child before I came, and God will never have another child." Jesus never said any such thing. However, Jesus was continually saying, and it's in the Bible, "I and my Father are one." (John 10:30)

Everything that Jesus said about himself is the truth of you. He came to show us what Divine Sonship is like. He came to show us what it means to be God's son, to be God's child. He came to demonstrate our Divine Sonship to us.

The only begotten son of God is the one relationship which everyone has with God.

But it is not enough for Jesus to demonstrate Divine Sonship. *It is the possibility and the responsibility of every person to come to the realization of his own Divine Sonship, just as Jesus did, and to demonstrate that Divine Sonship.* In this way, believing you are the son of God saves you or delivers you from the experience of being a "son of a gun."

Whatever You Believe About Yourself Seals Your Destiny

Whatever you believe about yourself seals your destiny. Whatever you believe about yourself brings you success or failure. Whatever you believe about yourself saves you or sinks you. Ask yourself this question, "What do I believe about myself?"

Most people give external causes power over them. They say, "Well, I don't succeed because of this, because of that, because of him or because of her." But only one thing saves you or sinks you, brings you success or failure, and that is what you believe about yourself. What you believe about yourself brings you salvation or damnation. What you believe about yourself creates your heaven or your hell.

If you know God as your Father, then immediately this puts you in line to receive all of the goodness, all of the riches, and all of the blessings of God.

This is pure self-image psychology, and that is really what the Bible is all about. This is really what Jesus is about. Jesus came to show each person who he is in God, and who God is in him. Jesus didn't come just to show you that He was God's son and the only son of God. Jesus came to show you that you, too, are God's child. Jesus came to show you that you, too, are one with the Father.

You Are Not A "Son Of A Gun," You Are The Son Of God!

Notice these words of Scripture, "If you believe not that I am He, you will die in your sins." (John 8:24) This means if you do not believe in your Divinity, you will suffer in the false sense of human self. If you do not believe that you are God's child, then you put yourself into the hands of negativity.

But if you know God as your Father, then immediately this puts you in line to receive all of the goodness, all of the riches, and all of the blessings of God. Because you will never receive all the good that belongs to you until you confess your Divine Sonship. This is the highest and the truest meaning of "confessing Christ" as the Christians put it.

A "son of a gun" is slang indicating one who does not know his Divine Parentage, or one of mean parentage.

The Prodigal Son

Remember what happened to the Prodigal Son? He left his father's house, but he was still his father's son. What this really means is that he left the consciousness of the Father. In his mistaken belief, he separated himself in consciousness from the Father.

The only way that you can ever be separated from God, is in mistaken belief. When he forgot who he was and went into the far country, he suffered like a "son of a gun," didn't he? He caught hell. Here again, forgetting who you are, forgetting your Divine Self, forgetting your Divine Sonship, is the only thing that causes mankind to catch hell.

Only one thing saves you or sinks you, brings you success or failure, and that is what you believe about yourself.

The Bible tells us that the Prodigal Son came to himself. And when he came to himself, he returned to his father and his father accepted him joyfully. You should be able to look through all of that right there and see what was happening. When he came to himself, he went to his father, and his father said, "This is my son," and immediately ordered all of the riches of life to be conferred upon his son.

You see, he was always his Father's son. The relationship between the father and the son never changed. The father waited with outstretched arms and when his son returned, he said, "Bring for him the best robe, and put it on him." (Luke 15:22) The Prodigal Son returned to his father; he awoke in consciousness to see his true relationship with the Father. Your relationship with the Father never changes. You are and always will be a child of God.

75

The best robe belongs to you, a child of God. Call in the musicians, let's rejoice because you know your own divinity.

QUOTES TO REMEMBER

"Divine Sonship is the one relationship which every man has with God."   ~ Rev. Ike

"You have the same Father as Jesus Christ."   ~ Rev. Ike

"God is love; and he that dwells in love dwells in God and God in him."   ~ I John 4:16

"Strong beliefs win strong men, and then make them stronger."   ~ Walter Bagehot

AFFIRMATIVE TREATMENT

I AM a child of God! I AM divine!

I know that my Divine Sonship gives me the power to live and to demonstrate everything good in a divine way.

I am the walking, talking, living Presence of God.

I am the Son of God, and not a "son of a gun"!

Thank you, Father, for this gift of Divine Sonship!

REVIEW QUESTIONS

1. Explain the difference between the traditional concept of Jesus' relationship with God and the way Rev. Ike explains it in this lesson. What does Jesus' relationship with God have to do with all mankind?

2. Define "Divine Sonship," and "son of a gun." What is the highest meaning of "confessing Christ"?

3. How can you best demonstrate Divine Sonship?

4. Explain the Bible verse, "I and my Father are one." (John 10:30)

5. How does what you believe about yourself seal your destiny? Discuss this in terms of success or failure.

Chapter 14

WHAT IS YOUR FINANCIAL PSYCHOLOGY?

Dr. Frederick Eikerenkoetter

Set a watch, 0 Lord, before my mouth; keep the door of my lips.
Psalms 141:3

A feast is made for laughter, and wine makes merry: but money answers all questions. Ecclesiastes 10:19

A SCIENCE OF LIVING PRINCIPLE

Everything is a condition of the mind. The idea comes first and then the manifestation of that idea. You can't be, you can't do, and you can't have anything until you first have the idea of it in your mind.

I have discovered some very interesting psychological reasons why people have money problems. Your problems with money, or your abundance of money for that matter, begin with what I call your "financial psychology," which is your attitude toward money.

To determine your financial psychology, ask yourself, "What is my attitude toward money?" I've really never heard anybody probe into the psychological area of money much before Rev. Ike came along. As a matter of fact, that question, "What is my attitude toward money?" sounds rather strange. The average person would say, "Well, what the heck has that got to do with the fact that I don't have the money that I need?"

How Do You Feel About Money?

But let me tell you, your attitude toward money has *everything* to do with your experience of money. *Your attitude toward money will draw money to you or repel money from you.* Your positive attitude toward money will help to maneuver you into better positions of financial compensation. A negative attitude toward money can even cut you off from getting that job or that position that would bring you greater financial rewards.

As I so often teach you, *"Everything begins in the mind."* Money, like everything else, is a psychic vibration. In order to experience money as you should or any of the riches of life as you should, you have to be in tune with the good you want.

Your attitude toward money will draw money to you or repel money from you.

Are You Indifferent To Money?

As I have been dealing with people through this Ministry, I have discovered some interesting things about people and their attitudes toward money. Those who are indifferent toward money do not have a good relationship with it.

I counseled a very aristocratic lady in Beverly Hills, California recently. Her late husband left her a wealthy woman. But, she said, her money was getting away from her. She wondered why, so I listened to her. Within sixty seconds after she started talking, I sized her up. I discovered that the reason this lady's money was getting away from her was because she had an indifferent attitude toward money.

Someone who was interested in hiring this lady said to her, "How much money do you want for accepting this position?"

And she said to the person who wanted to hire her, "Well, I really don't know. It doesn't matter." I told her, "If you said that, that is exactly why your money is getting away from you." Don't ever give money the idea that it doesn't matter to you.

Your attitude toward money has everything to do with your experience of money.

This reminds me of a very brilliant young man who was in college, making all A's. During his junior year, he got a job at the college, working in the college radio station. He told me about it, and he was all excited. He told me all about the job and all about the responsibility he had assumed. I asked him, "Son, how much money are they paying you for that?" He said, "Oh, Rev. Ike, that doesn't matter, it doesn't really matter what they are paying me." Right there, I told him, "Don't be indifferent toward money, or you are going to have money problems." And sure enough, for about a year after this young man graduated from college, he had difficulty finding a job. There he was an honor college graduate and out of work.

Every once in a while, I would talk to this young man, and I would work with him to help him purge his indifferent attitude toward money. Finally, when he changed his attitude toward money, when he got rid of his indifference toward money, he got a good job and settled into society. But this shows you that your indifference toward money will give you problems.

Here's an affirmation about money that I want to give you that will cure your indifference toward money. Say to yourself, "My positive interest in money increases money in my life."

It is impossible to be indifferent toward money and have a good relationship with it.

Deal With Money as a Personality

Learn to deal with money as a psychological or psychic entity. Deal with money as a personality. The theologians, and the philosophers for that matter, have personified everything but money. For example, error has been personified as the devil. I personify money as a very beautiful, but very sensitive, aristocratic woman. I talk about money as if it were a person, because money is a psychic vibration. In some of my money sermons I've told you, "Money is just like a woman." There is an old Irish proverb which states, "Money swore an oath that nobody that did not love her should ever have her."

In the psychic area of life, money is a person. Money has a mentality. Money has emotions. Money has feelings, and if you hurt the feelings of money, she is going to stay away from you, or give you trouble, or both. You may personify money to yourself however you like — perhaps as a very sensitive and desirable man. Whichever way you personify money, if you start dealing with money on that basis, you will get a lot more money a lot faster!

Watch What You Say

Never speak lightly of money. Let me give you one of those statements that people always make about money without thinking, "Well, money isn't everything." Never say what money isn't. That expresses an indifference toward money. That expresses an indifferent attitude.

Never speak lightly of money. Money's feelings are easily insulted, and she will go the other way. She will stick her head in the air and turn her nose up at you, and "ease on down the road" to someone who wants her.

Money Is Knocking At Your Door

Whatever you are indifferent toward will be indifferent toward you. Watch what you say about money. This is why the Psalmist said, "Set a watch, O Lord, before my mouth; keep the door of my lips." (Psalms 141:3) If people could only see how they talk money away from them. The truth is that money is knocking at your door. If it has to knock more than once, it'll go knock where someone will let it in the first time.

What you are indifferent toward will be indifferent toward you.

The goodness of life is knocking at your door. Success, prosperity, and happiness are knocking at your door. But you cannot be indifferent to the riches of life in any form and think that they are going to stick around you if they don't feel welcome. Who likes to stay around where they don't feel welcome? If money does not feel welcome with you, if you do not establish a welcome psychology for money, you are going to have problems with it.

Develop Your Financial Psychology

Sometimes these good religious people who have so much piety think they are above money. Never think that you are above money. That's a very subtle danger that you have to watch. Money is not everything, but it is like the old song says, "Money won't buy everything it's true, but what it won't buy, I can't use."

Make sure you have a positive "financial psychology" toward money and toward all the other riches of life: health, happiness, love, success, and prosperity. Don't be indifferent toward any good. Once you have a positive financial psychology, you will have an abundance of money in your life. But be careful to keep it in perspective. Don't be a servant to money. Don't serve money. Make sure money serves you. You are the master in your relationship with money. Be sure to use your money in constructive, positive ways.

QUOTES TO REMEMBER

"Your attitude toward money will draw money to you or repel money from you." ~ Rev. Ike

"Money swore an oath that nobody that did not love her should ever have her." ~ Irish Proverb

"When it is a question of money, everybody is of the same religion." ~ Voltaire

"Money is like a sixth sense — and you can't make use of the other five without it." ~ W. Somerset Maugham

AFFIRMATIVE TREATMENT

MONEY! I'm calling you into my life! I know you hear me!

Right here and right now, I'm telling you. Money, YOU love me!

You are welcome in my hands, in my pockets, and in my life all the time!

I open my heart and my mind to money in all forms — banknotes, certificates of deposit, stocks, and bonds.

I open my life to money through my loving, appreciating attitude.

Money knows I have the right financial psychology and loves me in return.

Money serves me in Divine right ways.

Money is my obedient servant.

I do not serve money, money serves me.

Money is wonderful stuff, and I let it multiply in my life.

Thank you, God-in-me, for money!

REVIEW QUESTIONS

1. What does Rev. Ike mean by the term "financial psychology"? Discuss negative and positive financial psychology.

2. What does your attitude toward money have to do with your experience of money? Explain.

3. Describe how you personify money and how this personification will make you better able to deal with money.

4. Discuss your own individual "financial psychology" and what you can do to improve it.

5. Why is it important to realize "Money is my servant. I am not the servant of money"?

Chapter 15

WILL THE REAL JESUS PLEASE STAND UP?

FOR EASTER

Dr. Frederick Eikerenkoetter

...The works that I do shall you do also, and greater works.
John 14:12

A SCIENCE OF LIVING PRINCIPLE

Christ is the Presence of God-in-man — every man.

Throughout the centuries, many different concepts of Jesus have been held by people all over the world. You can trace the development of these different concepts by walking through a museum and observing the different sculptures and paintings of Jesus. Some artists show Jesus as an innocent cherub; others as a frail, weak figure. But from everything I've read in the Gospels about Jesus, Jesus is a powerful personality! Nothing weak and sissified about Him at all!

Jesus Was a Powerful Personality

The Gospel tells us that Jesus spoke with authority. We are told that before the Crucifixion, the angry mob came at night with torches to find Him. And when they found Him, He was praying in the garden. The leaders of the mob demanded of Him, "Who are you? We're looking for Jesus!" And Jesus spoke these simple words: "I am He." And when Jesus said those words, the angry mob fell back.

Now let me tell you something about these words, "I AM." They are powerful. In fact, "I AM" is the most powerful affirmation you can make. Why? Because every time you say, "I AM," you are announcing the God Presence and the God Power within you. When Jesus said, "I AM He," these words were so full of God Power and God Presence that the mob fell back. Now does this sound like a weak-kneed, cowardly man? These are not the words of a weakling! These are the words of a powerful, towering personality!

On another occasion when Jesus was speaking, some officers were sent to arrest Him. And when they heard Him speak, they couldn't find it within themselves to arrest Him. So they returned without Jesus to those who had sent them. And the people who had sent them asked, "Why didn't you arrest Jesus? We sent you to get Him, we sent you to bring Him in." And they replied, "Never a man spoke like this."

Are You Relating To A "Sunday School Jesus"?

Now that we see that Jesus is a powerful personality, a towering personality, let's move on to another concept of Jesus and examine it. Are you still relating to a "Sunday School Jesus"? Do you remember back in Sunday School when we would sing the song, "Gentle Jesus, Meek And Mild"? That meek and mild concept is what I call the "Sunday School Jesus." And if you're still holding on to a Sunday School Jesus, I have news for you. There's no way for you to read in the Gospel about the life of Jesus and come up with a Jesus who was **always** meek and mild.

Now being mild is a positive trait to have, but sometimes you have to be strong, too. For example, the Gospel tells us that Jesus spoke bluntly concerning religious pretenders. On occasion He would say, "Oh, you generation of vipers!" Does that sound like a gentle Jesus, meek and mild? On another occasion, He cried out, "Oh, you scribes and Pharisees and hypocrites!" Does that sound like a gentle Jesus, meek and mild?

On one occasion Jesus really got mad. He went into the Temple and found the money changers in there, trying to merchandise

84

spiritual things. And He actually whipped those people out of the Temple shouting to them all the while, "My house shall be called a House of Prayer! Don't make my Father's House a house of merchandise!" Does this sound like a gentle Jesus, meek and mild? Of course not! **Jesus recognized that there is a time to act firmly and a time to speak firmly.**

Turn the Other Cheek

Now I want to go into this a little deeper, because a lot of you have this so-called Christian hang-up about being meek and mild. When Jesus said, "turn the other cheek," He did not mean if someone belts you on one side of your face that you should turn the other side and let him belt you on that side, too. He didn't mean for you to let people walk all over you and step on you.

You don't help yourself and you don't help anybody else by letting other people run over you! You have to let people know what you stand for and what you will not stand for. Draw the line like Jesus did. You should be kind, you should be compassionate, but you should not let people run over you! Because the same Jesus that was mild and loving, that had compassion and healed the sick... that was the same Jesus that drew the line and grabbed a whip and beat those merchandisers out of the Temple.

Learn To Talk Strong

It might surprise you to know it, but I believe in "strong talk." Jesus did it, I do it, and you should do it sometimes, too. But you have to know when and how. There is a time when you should be definite and positive with everybody. And in the long run, people will appreciate you more and respect you more if they know that you mean business.

Jesus Is the Ever-Living Presence of God Within

To some people, Jesus was a man on earth two thousand years ago, who is coming again "someday." But I say that Jesus represents the ever-living Presence of God within.

I'd like to share with you the Science of Living definition of Jesus Christ. Christ is the Presence of God-in-man — every man. Jesus is one who perfectly demonstrated the Christ. But it is not enough for Jesus to be the ONLY one to realize and demonstrate the Christ. Each man must come to know the truth of his own Christhood and demonstrate the Christ exactly as Jesus did.

Jesus realized who He was in God, and who God was in Him. And whenever Jesus said, *"I and my Father are one,"* He spoke the truth for every man and of every man. Jesus said, "I AM in the Father and the Father is in ME." And He demonstrated the Presence of God within Him, by healing, and blessing, and showing love to the whole world.

Jesus represents the realization and the demonstration of the Presence of God-in-man. When you realize that "I AM WHAT JESUS IS," then you can begin to demonstrate and do the works which Jesus did. For Jesus Himself said to His disciples, *"The works that I do shall you do also, and greater works."* (John 14:12) And the truth of every man is *"Thou art the Christ, the Son of the Living God."* (Matthew 16:16)

The purpose of Jesus is to show you that you are God's Son. When you believe in your Divine Sonship, this "saves" you from "sin" [error]. The purpose of the example of Jesus is to show each man his own Divine Sonship. Jesus portrays the true relationship of every man in God.

QUOTES TO REMEMBER

"God is the REAL man in me."   ~ Rev. Ike

"We have constantly to remember the   ~ Albert
inexorable Law; that we can only bring so   Schweitzer
much of the Kingdom of God into the world
as we possess within us."

"Behold, the kingdom of God is within you."   ~ Jesus
                                                (Luke 17:21)

AFFIRMATIVE TREATMENT

Right here and right now I recognize the Truth of me.

I know "I AM WHAT JESUS IS," the Christ, the Son of the Living God.

Christ is the Presence of God-in-me.

Christ is the Power of God-in-me.

The same God Power that Jesus had is in me.

The same healing and blessing power that Jesus had is in me.

I know who I am in God and who God is in me.

Thank you, Father.

Thank you, God-in-me.

REVIEW QUESTIONS

1. How is Jesus portrayed in the Bible?

2. Discuss the meaning of the words "Jesus" and "Christ."

3. Discuss the various concepts of Jesus.

4. Explain the meaning of "Turn the other cheek."

5. What is the purpose of the example of Jesus? What does the example of Jesus teach mankind?

Chapter 16

YOU ARE
YOUR SELF-AWARENESS

Dr. Frederick Eikerenkoetter

Be it done for you as you desire. Matthew 15:28

Let the weak say, I am strong. Joel 3:10

A SCIENCE OF LIVING PRINCIPLE

Faith is not something which is blind. Faith is not some abstract belief. Faith is what you believe about yourself. Whatever you believe about yourself, so be it unto you.

I teach what I call Mind Power. Some people have not been taught how to work their minds. Pardon the expression, but they were taught to work their behinds. I teach people that "the more you learn to work your mind, the less you have to work your behind!" And this is really what the Science of Living is all about.

Positive Self-Image Psychology

Positive self-image psychology is seeing oneself In one's own mind being, doing, and having the good one desires. If I could describe my teaching, my philosophy, in one term most succinctly, it would be "positive self-image psychology." And positive self-image psychology is what we all need. It's not a matter of one race needing it and another race needing something else. We all need positive self-image psychology. An old Greek philosopher said, "Man, know thyself." And that's just another way to say the same thing.

In this philosophy, which I also call the "science of positive self-awareness," I teach the individual to define his ideals and to project his ideals into reality by means of visualization, affirmation, and meditation. This is using Mind Power. This is "the Stuff I use!"

Positive self-image psychology is what we all need.

Define Yourself

Define what you want to be, what you want to do, and what you want to have. When I first started counseling people, it surprised me to find that there were so many people — people of all ages — who didn't know what they wanted out of life. When I asked them, "Well, what do you want to be?" they would say, "I don't know." "What do you want to do?" "I don't know." "What do you want to have?" "I don't know."

The individual must come to a point of self-definition and positive self-awareness. Here again, while speaking to students at the University of Alabama, they said to me, "Rev. Ike, I want you to tell me how to get a Cadillac. I want you to tell me how to get a million dollars."

In the Science of Living, we teach that if you want to be something, first see yourself in your mind being it. Define yourself as the one who is doing that which you want to do. Define yourself as the one who is having that which you want to have. And then visualize. See yourself in the theater of your own mind being, doing, and having the good which you desire. Also, you must use the technique of affirmation. You must affirm that you are that which you desire.

Add Good Things to "I AM"

I interpret the Bible psychologically, rather than theologically. One of the prophets in the Bible said, "Let the weak say, I AM strong." (Joel 3:10) Now, let's talk about these mystical words. "I 'AM." Whatever you add to "I AM," that is what you become. That's why I am against anybody teaching the so-called poor people to say, "I am poor." You know, it has become somewhat popular, it has become somewhat of a stylish cliché, if you please, to say, "poor people." If you don't want to be poor people, stop defining yourself as "poor people." Define yourself as prosperous. When you say, "I am poor," that is your self-definition. That is your self-awareness — and you are never going to be able to experience anything better than, or anything other than, your own self-definition.

Watch Out For Labels

Whatever you want to be, define yourself as that. If you're poor and you want to stay poor, keep saying, "I am poor." And don't grumble because you are poor. You have to reject all of the nice, neat, sociological labels which are passed down by the experts, including the experts from Washington. You know, they have some nice, neat labels in Washington to stamp on to people's foreheads. The label "poor people" is a famous one. That is the most negative self-image psychology that there is. Then there's another nice, neat label, "culturally deprived." But anybody who has been exposed to my Ministry can no longer claim he is "culturally deprived."

Whatever you add to "I AM" that is what you become.

It is a great disfavor to people to teach them this kind of negative self-image psychology. Because whatever you define yourself as, that is what you become. And the only way that you are going to become something else, or become what you want to be, is to redefine yourself as that which you want to become.

Change Your Circumstances

I want to quote the mystical words of the Apostle Paul from the Bible, the world's greatest book of psychology. He wrote to the Romans, in the twelfth chapter of his Epistle, "Be you transformed by the renewing of your mind." And I would like to quote further from that verse of Scripture. He said to the Romans, "Be you not conformed to this world." My interpretation of this is, "Do not conform to things as they appear." Do not be a slave to the conditions that you are in. Do not be locked in and bound by the undesirable circumstances that you find yourself in.

Change your circumstances by changing your self-image, by changing your self-definition. The Bible says, "Let the weak say, I AM strong." I like to add to that, "Let the poor say, I AM rich. Let the sick say, I AM well." This is redefining oneself. Let the weak one redefine himself as strong. Let the poor one redefine himself as rich, and so on.

See yourself in the theater of your own mind being, doing, and having the good that you desire.

What You Say Is What You Get

One of the things that I will never forget is the case of a thirteen-year-old boy who was brought here from Jamaica, British West Indies. All of his life he had suffered with asthma. He couldn't go to school very regularly because of his asthmatic condition.

The very first Sunday that he came to United Church in New York City he sat in the congregation. And before the service, I walked down the aisle as I usually do to meet and greet the people. This youngster leaned over from his seat and said to me in the wheezing tone of an asthmatic, "Reverend, please pray for me, I have asthma." I stopped for a moment and looked at him and then I said to him, "Son, I see in you a boy who has no asthma." Then I proceeded down the aisles to speak to other people.

I didn't talk to this young man again for about six months, but every Sunday after that I would see him sitting in the congregation, smiling. Finally, when I got a chance to talk to him, he told me a wonderful story. He said to me, "Rev. Ike, that Sunday when you walked down the aisles, I asked you to pray for me, because I had asthma. And when you said to me, 'Son, I see in you a boy who has no asthma,' something lifted from my chest, and I've never suffered with asthma since."

Change your circumstances, your conditions, by changing your self-image, by changing your self-definition.

Picture What You Want

What was it that I did that healed him? I redefined that young man's self-image for him. You have to give yourself a positive self-image that will lift you, that will heal you, that will prosper you. When I said to that young man, "Son, I see in you a boy who has no asthma," he immediately got in his mind a picture of himself as being healthy, as having no asthma, and he experienced that which he saw. You have to learn to use positive self-awareness to heal yourself, to bless yourself, and to prosper yourself. You have to learn to develop a positive self-awareness to become a winner in the game of life.

QUOTES TO REMEMBER

"Self-image is the key to everything." ~ Rev. Ike

"Take the place and attitude which belong to you, and all men acquiesce ~ Ralph Waldo Emerson

"The more you learn to work your mind, the less you have to work your behind." ~ Rev. Ike

"Chance favors only the mind that is prepared." ~ Louis Pasteur

AFFIRMATIVE TREATMENT

Right here and right now, I am constructing a positive self-image.

I see myself, in the theater of my mind, being, doing, and having all the good I desire.

I AM healthy! I AM happy! I AM loving! I AM successful!

I AM prosperous!

I AM rich!

Thank you, Father!

Thank you, God-in-me!

REVIEW QUESTIONS

1. Define the term "faith."

2. What does it mean to redefine oneself? How can this help a person?

3. How does "self-image psychology" help you to be, to do, and to have the good you desire?

4. What will happen if you put a negative label on yourself?

5. Are there circumstances in your life you would like to change? How are you going to go about it?

6. Explain how your words affect your life.

7. Discuss the importance of having a good, positive self-awareness.

Chapter 17

FROM ORDINARY TO EXTRAORDINARY

Dr. Frederick Eikerenkoetter

With God all things are possible. Matthew 19:26

A SCIENCE OF LIVING PRINCIPLE

Separate the truth of a person from what he appears to be. Look all the way through what appears, and see him, his Divine Self, the Presence of God within him. See him as he really is. *There is only one true identity, and that is the Divine Self.*

For years, we have read the beautiful verse of Scripture, "With God all things are possible," (Matthew 19:26) and we have had it preached at us. I know it, I believe it, and I am living proof of it. But it is not enough for us to know that "With God all things are possible." We must learn to make that which is possible a reality.

Make Successes Out Of Your Possibilities

That which is possible is no good to us until we make it a reality. Ask yourself this question, "What are some of my possibilities?" Some people conclude that they don't have many possibilities, so they never look for them, never discover them, and never turn them into realities. People like that say to me, "Why, Rev. Ike, I don't have any talent. I don't have any gifts." But let me tell you — *everyone* has some talent, some possibility within, that he can turn into reality.

94

_____

You have some talent, some possibility within you that you can make into a reality.

_____

Some of the most unlikely people have done some of the most good. Some of the most unlikely people have become successful and rich!

There Was a Light in Thomas Edison's Mind

I just love to tell about Thomas Edison, because he is someone who discovered the possibilities within him and made them realities for the whole world. He was an ordinary man who became extraordinary.

Thomas Edison went to a church school where a minister was the headmaster. One day, the headmaster got so aggravated at Thomas that he wrote a note to Thomas' mother and sent him home with it. The note said, "Don't send this boy back here to school. His brains are addled and he cannot learn." From that point on, Thomas Edison's mother gave him what little formal education he got.

Thomas Edison did not accept the idea that his brains were addled and he couldn't learn. As far as that particular teacher was concerned, this boy was a hopeless case. He didn't have any ability. He didn't have any talent. But there was a light in Thomas Edison's mind. He went out and lit up the whole wide world and brought forth so many, many great inventions.

Years later, after Thomas Edison became wealthy and well-known, that same teacher wrote him a letter and said, "Dear Mr. Edison, I hope you remember me. I used to be your schoolmaster. Now I'm old and on the retired list and don't get much money. Since you are now so wealthy and famous, I was wondering if you would help me?" Thomas Edison sent him twenty-five dollars, probably twenty-five dollars more than I would have sent him. I would have sent him a nice letter, however.

That which is a possibility is no good to us until we make it a reality.

God Guided Dr. George Washington Carver

Dr. George Washington Carver, a black man, growing up and working under the most disadvantageous conditions, discovered the talents that were in him, and brought forth many inventions. He said he would just walk across a field and ask God to guide him. God would guide him to pick up some ordinary element from the earth, like a peanut or a sweet potato. The eye of God through him would see so many unusual things in that ordinary element. Out of the peanut, for example, he made over three hundred products like soap and ink — products you might be using every day and not even know it. From the ordinary sweet potato, he made one hundred eighteen products, like flour, shoe blacking, and candy! So many different things he brought forth from ordinary, everyday foods. He was an ordinary man who became an extraordinary man. And in those days, who would have thought that a black man, particularly, would become extraordinary?

All things are possible, but until you make them into realities, they are of no use to you.

From An Asthmatic to a Great Outdoorsman

Theodore Roosevelt is another example of someone who developed the possibilities within him into realities. Theodore Roosevelt became a Rough Rider and the 26th President of the United States. But he was born very sickly and very weak. The doctors said that he would never live to manhood. He was an asthmatic when he was a baby and when he was a boy. Many nights, his father would take him in his arms and walk the floor with him, or walk out in the park with him wrapped in a blanket to try to help him get some fresh air in his lungs.

One day Theodore Roosevelt's father just sat him down and said to him, "Now if you really have the will and the desire to live and to be well, you can." Young Theodore had the will to live. He exercised himself and became quite an outdoorsman. He became an extraordinary man. When one of the great men of his day heard that he had later died in his sleep, he remarked, "That's the only way that death could take him, just sneak up on him while he was asleep."

When anyone around you tries to talk you down, tries to discourage you from developing possibilities within you, don't listen to them.

Everybody Called Henry Ford a Fool

Henry Ford is another of my saints. My saints are different from yours perhaps. Henry Ford is one of the saints of the Science of Living.

If you looked at Henry Ford, there was nothing about him which would give you the idea that, "Well, this man is going to become a billionaire." Stop and think about it. Not a millionaire, but a *billionaire*. Henry Ford, who really put the world on wheels, was a common, ordinary man. He had no visible talents, and no one told him he had great possibilities.

He worked on his little gasoline engine, and at one point in the process, he held the little contraption over the sink in the kitchen while his wife dripped the gasoline into the engine. He got a dentist to make the first spark plug. When he finally got the little contraption so that it would run, everybody in his neighborhood and in his village, called him a fool. Preachers called the automobile the "devil's horse." But now they all ride in one.

Don't listen to anyone's negative talk.

Both in the case of Edison and in the case of Ford, they didn't pay any attention when preachers, teachers, or anyone else tried to talk them down. When anyone around you tries to talk you down, tries to discourage you from developing the possibilities within you, don't listen to them. Don't listen to anyone's negative talk. Don't pay any attention to anyone who is trying to talk you down.

Ordinary People

I find one mistake that people make is this: They seem to think that extremely successful people, extremely wealthy people, are perhaps extremely gifted. But even a brief and superficial inspection of the subject will reveal to you that this is not so. The fantastic inventions that have come forth in this world have come forth, to a great degree, from ordinary people. People, who nobody thought had any talents or possibilities within them, have made their mark on the world in positive, wonderful ways.

Go to the library and read up on the lives of the great inventors and the great, successful people, and let each of their stories be an inspiration to you. It would surprise you that many of these people were ordinary. And not only were most of these people ordinary, some of these people became the very opposite of what conditions said they could be.

The fantastic inventions that have come forth in this world have come forth, to a great degree, from ordinary people.

So decide what you want to be, to do, and to have. Open your mind to the idea that you can make reality out of possibility. *Within you is the Presence and Power of God.* This is your true self. Look to the Presence and Power of God within to make that which is possible a reality, and you too will become extraordinary.

QUOTES TO REMEMBER

"There is only one true identity and that is the Divine Self."   ~ Rev. Ike

"The reward of a thing well done, is to have done it." ~ Ralph Waldo Emerson

"They can because they think they can." ~Virgil

"Thinking is the hardest work there is, which is the probable reason why so few engage in it." ~ Henry Ford

AFFIRMATIVE TREATMENT

Right here and right now, I open my mind to all the great possibilities within me.

Through the Presence of God-in-me, all things are possible.

The mind of God-in-me gives me great ideas which prosper me and make me successful.

The mind of God-in-me is always giving me new and better ideas for making money.

I see myself with an abundance of money in my hands, in my pocketbook, in my bank accounts.

Through the Presence of God-in-me, I know it is possible to enjoy all the riches of life: health, happiness, love, success, prosperity, and money.

Thank you, God-in-me!

REVIEW QUESTIONS

1. Why is it not enough to know that "With God all things are possible"? What more must you do?

2. Do you have to be extremely gifted to be extremely successful and extremely wealthy?

3. Can you think of other ordinary people who did extraordinary things?

4. List some of your possibilities. How are you going to make them realities?

5. How should you regard other people's discouraging remarks toward you?

Chapter 18

GOD HAS GIVEN YOU WINNING POWER

Dr. Frederick Eikerenkoetter

God has not given us the spirit of fear; but of power, and of love, and of a sound mind. II Timothy 1:7

A SCIENCE OF LIVING PRINCIPLE

Go forth every day with the attitude and feeling of a big-time winner.

God has given *you* the power to be a winner in the game of life. He has given you the ability to be as great as you want to be. Think about that for a moment. God's gift to you is the ability to make your life as you want it to be. He has given you the power to be what you want to be, to do what you want to do, and to have what you want to have.

I like the way Brother Paul said it, "God has not given us the spirit of fear; but of power, and of love, and of a sound mind." (II Timothy 1:7) This is a very important concept for you to understand. Once you understand it, once you accept it, once you get the spirit of it, you will be a winner in the game of life.

God has given you the ability to be as great as you want to be.

God's Gift to Us

There is an old spiritual that says, "I got shoes, you got shoes, all God's children got shoes." To me, that old spiritual means that God has given every one of His children a gift. And of course, when you understand this spiritually, you will understand that God has prepared every one of His children to win in the game of life.

God's gift to you is the ability to make your life as you want it to be.

I am reminded of a very successful executive who hired a new secretary. One day he told her to accomplish some particular task. "Oh, but that's impossible," the secretary said to him. So he replied, "I want you to go out there in the office and look in the dictionary. Look up the word 'impossible' and tell me what it means." The new secretary went out, looked in the dictionary, and came back with a puzzled expression on her face. She said to her boss, "Oh, Mr. So-and-so, somebody has cut out the word 'impossible' from this dictionary." "I did it," he said, "I got every dictionary and I turned to the word 'impossible,' and I clipped it out. So if you work for me, 'impossible' is not in your vocabulary."

Everything good is possible when you look to the Presence and Power of God within.

You Can!

Every time you say, "I can't," every time you *think*, "I can't," every time you *feel*, "I can't," you are denying the possibilities of God. Disbelieve all the reasons why you can't. Disregard what *seem* like reasons why you can't. Disregard your good excuses. That is the trouble with some of you, your excuses are too good! Look beyond all the reasons why you can't be, can't do, and can't have. Think about all that you can be, can do, and can have, and you will discover that you CAN. You CAN be a winner!

Excuses, Excuses!

On the wall in the lobby of United Church in New York City is a statement by Rev. Ike, "There is nothing so bad as a good excuse. And the better the excuse, the worse it is." I had my staff paste that statement up in every one of our offices. I had them paste that statement up in the kitchens at all the Episcopal residences of this church. I sent my instructions, "I want everybody who works for me to know that I don't want any excuses." I told them, "The better the excuse, the worse it is!"

There is nothing so bad as a good excuse. And the better the excuse, the worse it is.

Cleaning Man Really Cleans Up!

I want to share with you a very happy experience that I had on the streets of Beverly Hills, California. I was looking in the window of an elegant men's shop and a very well-dressed, handsome, business-like young black man came up to me and said, "Oh, Rev. Ike, I just want to tell you what your Ministry, what your teachings, have done for me." He said, "A few years ago, my father and I left Louisiana and came here to Los Angeles. When we arrived here, I had only twelve dollars. I got myself a job on a cleaning crew that cleans buildings. Then I saw you on television and I started listening to your teachings. I figured there was better for me. I heard you say, 'You can be what you want to be, you can do what you want to do, you can have what you want to have.' Rev. Ike, I believed what you said, and I started my own building cleaning company. I finally got to the point where I made five hundred dollars a month. I thought that was big stuff. But as I continued to use your teachings, as I developed my self-awareness, I became even more successful."

As we stood on that corner, he pointed out the big, high-class buildings he cleaned and told me about other large bank buildings all around the city of Los Angeles where he has cleaning contracts. He has his own maintenance crews. He said, "Rev. Ike, I can hardly believe it, but standing right here, today, I am making ten thousand dollars a month, thanks to your teachings and inspiration."

You can be what you want to be, do what you want to do, and have what you want to have, if you believe in the God-in-you.

Hallelujah!

That young man and I almost had a shouting meeting on the corner that morning. He was trembling with emotion. But when you let God get in you and work a miracle in your life, it just does something for you. He reads my Success Ideas that I write and send out every month, and I gave him the idea of prosperity; I gave him the idea that he can be and do and have. I gave him the idea that there were greater things for him. And, he believed it. As Rev. Ike says, "Ideas make millionaires."

One other beautiful thing he said to me was, "Rev. Ike, all of the white people in all of these high-class buildings that I have contracts with are glad to give me a chance and are glad to do business with me." If you really "get a tiger in your tank" and you believe in yourself correctly, if you get motivated and approach people with the right attitude, people will help you, no matter what your race.

Ideas make millionaires.

When this young man first came to Los Angeles with no money, he could have made excuses for not succeeding. He could have said, "I can't" to the idea of prosperity. Instead, he believed that through the Presence of God within, he could be, do, and have whatever good he desired. He knew that health, happiness, success, and prosperity were for him. He has what it takes because he uses what God put in him. He knows that through the Presence and Power of God in him, he will experience more success, more prosperity, and more money. This man has what it takes because God put it in him. I've got what it takes because God put it in me. *You've got what it takes because God put it in you.* Don't deny this God-Power in you.

Don't back away from your responsibility to use this power for your own good. Use it to get ahead. Use it to be a winner in the game of life.

QUOTES TO REMEMBER

"There is nothing so bad as a good excuse. And the better the excuse, the worse it is."   ~ Rev Ike

"There is nothing so bad as a good excuse. And the better the excuse, the worse it is."   ~ Anonymous

"The way to hell is paved with good excuses."   ~ Anonymous

AFFIRMATIVE TREATMENT

I have what it takes because God put it in me.

God's gift of health, happiness, love, success, and prosperity is in me.

I look to the Presence and Power of God-in-me for continued health, happiness, love, success, and prosperity.

Thank you, Father!

Thank you, God-in-me!

REVIEW QUESTIONS

1. What are some of the powers God has given you?

2. What lesson can be learned from the story about the executive who cut the word "impossible" out of the dictionary?

3. Every time you say or think or feel, "I can't," what are you doing to yourself?

4. Explain why there is nothing so bad as a good excuse.

5. Write down some of the ways in which you are going to use the winning power God has given you. Be specific.

Chapter 19

HOW SWEET IT IS!

FOR MOTHER'S DAY

Dr. Frederick Eikerenkoetter

My meditation of Him shall be sweet: I will be glad in the Lord. Psalms 104:34

Where there is no vision, the people perish. Proverbs 29:18

A SCIENCE OF LIVING PRINCIPLE

You are responsible for making every day a happy day. When God individualized Himself in you, He gave you the power, the ability, to have all the good you desire.

If you were to stop and think positively for a moment of all the wonderful, beautiful things in your life, you might be surprised at how many blessings you have. I love that wonderful old Christian hymn that says, "Count your blessings, name them one by one." If you do that, it will surprise you.

Whenever you have a good experience, whenever you enjoy something, say to yourself, "How sweet it is!" Whenever you have a chance to celebrate with your family or with your friends, even when you sit down to a good meal, stop and be thankful. Declare with your heart, "How sweet it is!"

The Sweetness of Life

That is a wonderful way to express your attitude toward life, "How sweet it is!" And it is a good way to express thanks. It may not seem a very religious way to some of you, but whenever good things happen to you, whenever good things come your way, just say, "How sweet it is!" When you learn to think about the good things that you're always enjoying, when you begin to get the outlook and the attitude of "How sweet it is," you will find that your life will get sweeter and sweeter.

If you want to experience the sweetness of life, you have to let your attitude toward life be, "How sweet it is!"

Take Positive Action

As long as you are a chronic complainer, you are never going to find the sweetness of life. Any time you catch yourself getting into a rut, complaining, watch out. Get a hold of yourself and say, "Wait a minute, here. I have complained long enough. I have wrung my hands and whined long enough. I have complained to everyone there is to complain to. I have complained about everyone there is to complain about. I have complained about everything there is to complain about. Now, what positive action am I going to take? What positive action am I going to take to make things as I want them to be?'"

There is a difference between what is called "constructive criticism" and complaining. Constructive criticism means that if you look at something and it does not come up to standards, you devise ways and means of correcting it. Think positive thoughts; take positive action! This business of just complaining about everything is no good. I know some people who wouldn't be happy unless they had something to complain about. The more you complain, the more you will have to complain about. Let your attitude toward life be, "How sweet it is!"

Count Your Blessings

In order to have the good which you desire, get in the habit of counting your blessings. The more you begin to appreciate the good you have, the more good you will have to appreciate. The more you praise the Lord, the more you will have to praise the Lord for. The more you become conscious of having good, and being good, and doing good, the more good will come into your life. Count your blessings. Declare, "How sweet it is!"

The more you begin to appreciate the good you have, the more good you will have to appreciate.

There are so many sweet things in life to appreciate — so many "plums." Plums, you know, represent major benefits. Have you ever heard the expression, "Oh, he got a plum"? Maybe an executive got a promotion and all the other executives got together and said, "He got a plum." Plums represent the major benefits in life, major good coming your way.

"Write the Vision..."

This reminds me of a few lines from an old Christmas poem:

> The children were nestled
> all snug in their beds,
> While visions of sugar plums
> danced in their heads....

You know I always look for the principles behind everything — and the symbols in this verse will help me make my point. As I've said, sugar represents the sweetness of life. "The children were nestled all snug in their beds" indicates that the conscious, reasoning mind is put to rest while you use your imagination to create and to "see" things as you want them to be. That's why I tell you that the best time to visualize is just before you go to sleep at night.

Always go to sleep with "visions of sugar-plums" dancing in your head. Go to sleep seeing and feeling yourself being, doing, and having the good which you desire. While you are asleep, your destiny is arranged in the subconscious. Learn to "dream dreams and see visions." Learn to thrill to the vision of yourself being, doing, and having the good which you desire.

Get It In Your Head

Now let me ask you what dances in your head? What ideas fill your mind? Whatever ideas you have in your head are what you are going to get in life. Something is always dancing in your head. Is it good? Is it bad? Is it negative? Is it positive? Does it make for health or does it make for sickness? Does it make for prosperity or does it make for poverty? What's dancing in your head?

Whatever ideas you have in your head are what you are going to get in life.

Be sure you know what's "dancing in your head." When you have only sweetness and good dancing in your head, you will experience sweetness and goodness in your life. "How sweet it is!"

QUOTES TO REMEMBER

"Life meets you like you meet life."   ~ Rev. Ike

"How sweet it is!"   ~ Jackie Gleason

"The more you begin to appreciate the good   ~ Rev. Ike
you have, the more good you will have to
appreciate."

"Human beings can alter their lives by   ~ William James
altering their attitudes."

AFFIRMATIVE TREATMENT

I now enter the theater of my mind and shut the door to the world-mind.

I open my inner eye and look to the stage of my imagination. Look who's dancing in my head! It's me!

I see myself as I want to be — healthy and whole in body, mind, and spirit.

I see myself doing exactly what I want to do.

I see myself having exactly what I want to have. I am appreciating all the good things in my life. How sweet it is!

Thank you, Father.

Thank you, God-in-me!

REVIEW QUESTIONS

1. Why are praise and thanksgiving important? What do they multiply?

2. What effect does the complaining habit have?

3. What is the difference between mere complaining and constructive criticism?

4. What does the process of visualization help you do? When is the best time in the day to visualize?

5. Explain the meaning of "visions of sugar-plums dancing in their heads."

Chapter 20

THE MENTAL EQUIVALENT

Dr. Frederick Eikerenkoetter

Arise, walk through the land in the length of it and in the breadth of it; for I will give it unto you. Genesis 13:17

A SCIENCE OF LIVING PRINCIPLE

Whatever you want, you must first have the idea of it in your mind. If you have the idea and if you have faith in that idea, then it shall manifest itself in your experience.

A few years ago, I was in a Rolls Royce showroom in San Francisco looking at some of those nice Rolls Royces. A young man who was also looking at those Rolls Royces recognized me and came over to meet me. He said to me, "Rev. Ike, I want you to pray for me so that I can get this Rolls Royce." I decided to be rather blunt with him, and simply said, "I will not, because you are not ready for it!" Now that might sound rather harsh to you, so let me explain.

Are You Mentally Prepared?

You already have everything that you are ready for. If you don't have something, you are not ready for it. You might think you are, but mentally, you are not.

The late Emmet Fox used the term "mental equivalent" to refer to this same principle. It means that before you can have anything, you must first have the *idea* of it in your mind. We are both saying the same thing, only with different words.

You can only have objectively that which you have the mental equivalent of subjectively.

Are You Imprisoned By Your Circumstances?

Whatever good you want, first possess the idea of it in your mind. Never mind what you don't have objectively. This is where people get hung up so many times. People get so hung up on what they *don't have*, that it kills their creative power to think about what they *can have*. People are so hung up on "I can't be" and "I don't have." They are really hung up on "I don't have."

A young lady once said to me, "Rev. Ike, don't tell me to say I'm rich when I don't have any money! I don't have any money and don't tell me to say anything different!" But if all you can do is think of your present circumstances, then you imprison yourself in your present circumstances.

Whatever good you want, first possess the idea of it in your mind.

You must *feel* the idea of the good you desire in your mind, in your heart. Let me give you some plain, practical, capitalistic examples. If you want a new house, you must first of all have the idea of that new house in your mind. You must possess the *mental equivalent* of that house in your mind. This is why I teach you to visualize, to go into the theater of your mind, and see yourself walking into that new house. Go to the refrigerator, open the door and get a snack out of it. See yourself drinking your favorite beverage, whatever it is, out of that refrigerator. Go into your new bedroom and stretch out on your mattress.

Many times, in a visualization treatment, I will send you to the wall where the safe is, behind the drapery. Open up that safe and see all the money, the jewels and the bank books you desire. See yourself having all the good you desire. All of this mental activity, which I call visualization, helps you develop the mental equivalent of the good that you desire.

You already have everything you are ready for.

Behold the Good You Desire

You remember in Genesis, the Lord told Abraham to lift up his eyes and "...walk through the land the length of it and the breadth of it; for I will give it unto you." (Genesis 13:17) What does this mean? This means that whatever good you can see and feel and have the mental equivalent of will come to you. The Presence and Power of God-in-you will provide.

Everything That You Are Ready For Is Ready For You

I preached a sermon once and I used these words: "Everything that you are ready for is ready for you." You now have everything that you are ready for. Whatever you don't have, you don't have it because you are not ready for it, you don't have the mental equivalent of it yet. And that is why I teach you to raise your consciousness, to develop the mental equivalent of the increasing good that you desire. That is why I tell you that when you want something, write it down. "Write the vision and make it plain." (Habakkuk 2:2) It helps you build the mental equivalent of the good you desire.

Raise your consciousness to develop the mental equivalent of the increasing good that you desire.

Many times when people say to me, "Rev. Ike, pray for me to get such-and-such a thing," I'll ask them bluntly, "Are you ready for it?" They usually say, "Oh yes." And I say, "Oh no, you're not. Because if you were ready for it, you would have it." You have, right now, exactly what you're ready for. You have, right now, exactly what your mind can accommodate and so have I.

I have made this following statement before, "The amount of money that you have exactly matches your mental readiness for money." If you only have a little money, you are only ready for a little. You only have the mental equivalent of a little money. People will swear up and down, "Oh yes, I'm ready for a lot more money." But that is simply the intellect talking. You know what they mean when they say that they're ready for it. They mean that the idea of having it blows their minds. It is not much deeper, however, than wishful dreaming. And I don't want you to think that what I'm dealing with here is just some type of wishful dreaming. I'm not trying to teach you wishful dreaming, I'm teaching you positive visualization. And there is a difference. Positive visualization is seeing and feeling the good you desire in the depth of your subconscious mind. Wishful dreaming is just idle wishing without really believing.

You have, right now, exactly what you're ready for. You have, right now, exactly what your mind can accommodate.

You Can Only Get That Which You Already Have

Whenever you have a good desire that comes into your mind, ask yourself this question: "Do I have the mental equivalent of this?" And then go to work, immediately, in building the mental equivalent in your consciousness.

You can only get that which you already have. You cannot have what you do not have. You cannot acquire what you do not already have in your mind as a mental equivalent. Once you establish in your mind the mental equivalent of the good you desire, it will come to you. It will be drawn to you and you will be drawn to it. What may seem to you, on the objective level, like happenstance, will be your own mind power, connecting you with the right people, the right events, the right modus operandi for achieving your good purposes. Things will happen to you because you are mentally prepared. Good things will happen to you because you have the consciousness, the correct self-awareness, for the good that you desire.

I want to say it once again, and it sounds somewhat like a riddle: *You cannot have what you do not have.* You cannot get what you do not already have in your mind as a mental equivalent.

I've Got It!

There is a young boy in this Ministry who is now thirteen years of age. He first wrote to me and adopted me when he was nine years of age. Many of you have seen him with me on television. His name is Marc Jefferson. A few years ago, he bought his mother a beautiful home with a swimming pool.

You cannot have what you do not have.

Good things began happening to Marc when he was nine years old. He had written me a letter and said, "Dear Rev. Ike, I want you to pray for me to get a job on television and in the theater so that I can buy myself some new clothes and buy my mother a house."

After he wrote me that letter, he went for a job interview. There were a lot of kids there that day, and he was one of the first children who was interviewed. When he came out, he looked at his mother and said, "I've got it." And his mother asked, "What do you mean? All of these other children here haven't been interviewed yet." But Marc said, "Oh, but I've got it."

They went home and he didn't hear anything about the interview for a few days. But every day when he came home from school for lunch, Marc would say to his mother, "Did the studio call yet? Well, that's all right. I've got it." About the third day, his mother said, "The studio called and you've got it." He was paid several hundred dollars a day to start. Pretty good for a little nine year old, isn't it? Notice what Marc said right after the interview: "I'VE GOT IT." He had the mental equivalent of what he wanted. He had it in his mind. He had it in his feelings.

All of this mental activity, which I call visualization, helps you develop the mental equivalent of the good that you desire.

I'm always amused by Marc. He bought a new car and sits in the back seat reading the *Wall Street Journal* while his mother chauffeurs him around. He tells his mother, "Stick with me, Mommy, I'll see you through. I'll take care of you."

Expose Yourself to the Good You Desire

I tell my congregation in New York, "Always buy the *Wall Street Journal*." Even if you don't know what it is all about, carry it with you. Your subconscious mind knows what it is, and will pick up a certain feeling, a certain mentality from it. Your subconscious mind knows that the *Wall Street Journal* is associated with high finance. This is why I tell you, also, to be sure to get those high-class, high-living magazines like *Town and Country*. If you don't want to read it all, just look at the pictures. Your subconscious mind understands all of this. All of this helps you to build a mental equivalent of money, affluence, opulence, and luxury. And whatever you have the mental equivalent of will come into your life.

QUOTES TO REMEMBER

"You can only get that which you already have."

~ Rev. Ike

"It is the mind that makes the body rich."

~ William Shakespeare

"Mind moves matter."

~ Virgil

"Man's work is an extension of himself. It is a revelation of himself. It is a revelation of his inner life, both to others and to himself."

~ Richard Lynch

"Undertake something that is difficult; it will do you good. Unless you try to do something beyond what you have already mastered, you will never grow."

~ Ronald Osborn

AFFIRMATIVE TREATMENT

I see myself being what I want to be.

I see myself doing what I want to do.

I see myself having exactly what I want to have.

I'm not taking whatever comes along!

I have decided what I want to be, to do, and to have, and I now see it in my mind.

I feel it. I establish the mental equivalent of it, right here and right now.

Thank you, Father!

Thank you, God-in-me!!! I've got it!

REVIEW QUESTIONS

1. What is the difference between "wishful dreaming" and positive visualization?

2. Define "mental equivalent."

3. Discuss what happens when you establish in your mind a "mental equivalent" of something.

4. What happens when you only think of your present circumstances?

5. Are you imprisoned by your circumstances? Discuss how. What are you going to do about it?

6. What does Rev. Ike mean when he says, "You can only have that which you already have"?

Chapter 21

DON'T LET THE STARS GET IN YOUR EYES

Dr. Frederick Eikerenkoetter

This is the day which the Lord has made; I will rejoice and be glad in it. Psalms 118:24

A SCIENCE OF LIVING PRINCIPLE

Let nothing outside of you control your destiny. Through the Presence of God within, you and only you can make your good desires come true.

The age-old custom of wishing on a star has become glamorized and computerized into big business today. But for all this sophistication, the results obtained from consulting and wishing on a star are pretty much the same — worthless!

What You Expect Is What You Get

It is interesting to me how many intelligent people will not start their day without first reading their horoscopes; or, as I like to call them, "horror-scopes." Horoscopes claim to predict the future. They presume to chart bad or unlucky days, periods of unfavorable business or personal relationships, and warnings against travel and spending money. They are certainly full of negative predictions.

One common horoscope prediction which seems to recur often, tells people to "avoid making decisions today." How can you possibly get dressed, go to work, or even decide what you want for lunch, if you pay attention to something telling you to "avoid decisions"?

Then, once in a great while, the "perfect day" is suggested for you to transact all your business, enhance your love life, and make the world a better place in which to live. Suddenly, the negative conditions are supposed to change, and when that doesn't happen, even your so-called "good days" end up in frustration.

The results obtained from consulting astrology and wishing on a star are pretty much the same — worthless!

Horoscopes which claim to predict positive and then negative experiences confuse the mind which, in turn, confuses the life experience. Suppose the horoscope said, "Today will be a bad day for you; you won't feel very well." But when you woke up in the morning, you were feeling fine, looking forward to working and seeing your friends. Now you read this horoscope which tells you that you will have a bad day. First thing you know, your head begins to ache and your knees feel weak. That horoscope programmed you for those aches and pains, and now you are experiencing them!

Thoughts are the food of the mind.

The Importance of Your Thoughts

Your experience is determined by the ideas in your mind. "Keep your heart [inner mind] with all diligence, for out of it are the issues of life." (Proverbs 4:23) When reading horoscopes, people are programming their minds to project what they have read into their experience. Once these negative thoughts are accepted by the mind, they become negative experiences. The Bible says, "As a man thinks, so is he." (Proverbs 23:7) As Rev. Ike says, "You are what you think, and thoughts are the food of the mind."

Tell Your Mind What to Think

It is important that you learn to rule your own mind. You must take the responsibility of telling your mind what to think. Too many people have their minds ruled from the outside in, instead of ruling their own minds from the inside out.

Horoscopes are just another device of the world-mind to tell you what to think. Starting today, take complete responsibility for telling your mind what to think. Only let in good, positive, decisive thoughts.

Change Your Sign

When people ask you what sign you are under, for heaven's sake don't tell them. People project all sorts of things for you according to what sign you are "under." It's all cut out for you. You don't have to think anything — your horoscope tells you what to think and what not to think, what to do and what not to do. If you mentally put yourself under any sign, you lose control of your own future. When people ask me what sign I was born under, I say "the dollar sign." That's a sign I understand! Then I add, "But I'm not under the signs, the signs are under me." So don't tell anybody your so-called sign.

Look To This Day

"This is the day which the Lord has made; I will rejoice and be glad in it." (Psalms 118:24) Every day is a day which the Lord has made ... so every day is a good day. When you wake up each day, repeat that Bible verse.

Don't look to the stars for the answer to what the future holds for you. Look within yourself. Look to the Presence and Power of God within.

Program your mind with positive thoughts before starting the day. Your body needs fuel in the form of food before you begin each day. And your mind needs positive thoughts before it begins each day.

Positive thoughts will program your mind for positive experiences throughout the day. "This is the day which the Lord has made… rejoice and be glad in it." Today is all we have. Yesterday is gone and tomorrow never comes.

Be Your Own Fortune Teller

Don't look to the stars for the answer to what the future holds for you. Look within yourself. Look to the Presence and Power of God within. Decide the good you want in your life and believe that through the Presence of God-in-you, it will come about.

Think carefully about all the good you want in your life. Decide exactly what good you want. Get it clearly in your mind. Acknowledge the Presence and Power of God within as your source. You will know what the future holds for you because you will be the one to determine it. Through the Presence of God-in-you, you can be what you want to be, you can do what you want to do, and you can have what you want to have!

QUOTES TO REMEMBER

"Thoughts are the food of the mind."   ~ Rev. Ike

"This is the day which the Lord has made; I   ~ Psalms 118:24
will rejoice and be glad in it."

"Self-reverence, self-knowledge, self-   ~ Alfred, Lord
control, these three alone lead life to   Tennyson
sovereign power."

"Today is all we have. Yesterday is gone   ~ Anonymous
and tomorrow never comes."

AFFIRMATIVE TREATMENT

Right here and right now I decide to be in control of my life and my future. I decide exactly what I want and get it clearly in my mind. I think good, positive thoughts.

Good positive thoughts make good positive days, and good positive life experiences.

Today and every day is the day the Lord has made, I shall rejoice and be glad in it.

Thank you, Father!

Thank you, God-in-me!

REVIEW QUESTIONS

1. Why does Rev. Ike call them "horror-scopes"?

2. Should you consult the stars, horoscopes, or astrology about the future? Why or why not?

3. Discuss how horoscopes can affect your life if you read them.

4. What does it mean to *"Keep your heart [inner mind] with all diligence, for out of it are the issues of life"?* — Proverbs 4:23

5. Discuss the advantages and disadvantages of determining your own future.

Chapter 22

A PUSH IN THE RIGHT DIRECTION

For Commencement Day

Dr. Frederick Eikerenkoetter

You shall decree a thing and it shall be established unto you; and the light shall shine upon your ways. Job 22:28

A SCIENCE OF LIVING PRINCIPLE

Give yourself a push — in the right direction! Acknowledge the Divine Presence, the Divine Power of God-in-you.

As I prepared the notes for this lesson, I was reminded of a young man whose career was not going as fast as he wanted it to go. And so I said to him, "You seem to be hesitating; what are you waiting for?" And he said, "Reverend, I'm waiting for someone to give me a push." Whereupon I sort of preached to him the whole lesson that I'm about to give you.

I said to him, "Son, you're going to have to learn how to give yourself a push!" And I want you to remember that!

In life you're going to have to give yourself a push. You can't just sit around waiting for somebody else to come along and help you do what you want to do, or give you a push in the right direction. Because if you wait for someone else to do that for you, life will just pass you by.

I Broke the Habit

Some years ago when I decided to begin this Ministry, I decided to write all the friends from my childhood preaching days ... a lot of people I had ministered to when I was a teenager who had gone on to become successful and prosperous. I said to myself, "I'll write them and ask them to give me a push. I'll write them and ask them if they will help me to begin this radio and television Ministry."

And so I wrote to these church members that had gone different places and gotten good jobs, and I told them what I wanted to do. And I waited for their letters back. And I waited, and I waited, and I didn't get a single letter. Nobody was willing to give me a push. I finally got one letter from one church, and they told me they couldn't help me.

Well, from that moment on, I was broken of the habit of waiting for someone else to come along and give me a push! From that moment on, I didn't wait for anybody to decide for me what I could and could not do!

Setting Positive, Definite Goals

In this lesson I want to teach you one of the most important things that you must do in order to give yourself a push in life. If you want to give yourself a push in the right direction you must first of all set definite goals for yourself.

If you want to live successfully and get the good which you desire, you must set goals. You must decide what you want! Get in the habit of deciding exactly what you want, and ask yourself, "What do I really want?" And visualize in your mind the good that you desire. Ask yourself, "What do I really want to be? What do I really want to do? What do I really want to have?" You'd be surprised to know how many people never really decide exactly what they want.

I had a very interesting experience recently in Detroit when a minister and his wife visited with me. His wife said to me,

"Oh Rev. Ike, I've heard all those testimonies about people in your Ministry getting cars and houses and money and all that. But you know, I've been praying for a car for the last two years and I still haven't got it! I've been probing my mind to try to find out why not, but I still don't know why." I just asked her one question. I said, "What kind of car do you want?" All of a sudden her face went blank. She said, "Uh, I really don't know." **I said, "That's why you haven't gotten it."**

Is Your Mind A Blank?

If you don't know what you want, if you have nothing definite in your mind, if your mind is a blank about the good you desire, that's exactly what you will get — nothing! I asked this lady again, "What kind of car do you want?" She finally said, "Well, any kind. It doesn't make a difference." And the thing about it, the woman works for General Motors! Yes, she does! She works for General Motors and she is a preacher's wife! If a preacher's wife working for General Motors in Detroit can't get a car, who can? I asked her at least three times, "What kind of car do you want?" She just kept saying, "I don't know, any kind. It doesn't matter." I said, "Now you see why you haven't gotten it."

Her husband was there and it dawned on him, too. His wife hadn't set definite goals. She didn't have a clear idea in her mind of what she wanted. I finally got her to say exactly what kind of car she wanted. And after she knew exactly what she wanted, I said to her, "Now go and get it." She began to say, "Well, how?" And I said, "Don't ask how. Just go and get it." She should have the car by now.

Be Choosy!

To give yourself a push in the right direction, you must set up positive goals for yourself, you must be decisive. You must decide definitely what you want to be, do, and have. Get a clear idea of the good you want in your mind. There is nothing that your mind will not do for you, if you tell it what you want! This is what the Psalmist meant when he sang out, *"My heart is fixed, O God, my heart is fixed."* (Psalms 57:7)

When you give yourself a push, it's important that you set goals. It's important that you decide exactly what you want. If you want something, never say, "Well, I don't know exactly what kind, it doesn't matter." Never say, "It doesn't matter." Any time you have a choice to make, make that choice decisively. Even when it comes to ice cream, I always make a definite choice. I was at one of the church residences in the mountains in California recently, and one of my aides said to me, "Reverend, what kind of ice cream do you want?" He said, "We have butter pecan, black cherry, strawberry, and vanilla. What kind do you want?" "Well," I said to myself, "Rev. Ike says you've got to make a choice. I can't say it doesn't make a difference." So I said, "I'm going to make a definite choice. Bring me all the flavors that you have. And give me a half scoop of each one."

Don't wait for anyone else to give you a push. Don't let anyone else make a choice for you. When you're offered a choice, never say, "Any kind." Never say, "It doesn't matter." Always make your own choice. I'm going to put it more clearly. "Be choosy!" If you get in the habit of just accepting anything, that's when people will just give you any old thing. Some of you wonder why you get such bad deals. It's because you don't make a choice, and people just give you any old thing, good quality or bad quality. Be choosy!

When you are giving yourself a push in life, be sure you know what you want. Be sure you tell your mind what you want. Then all the ways and means will begin to open for you.

QUOTES TO REMEMBER

"Give your mind a purpose, and your mind power will lead you to the fulfillment." ~ Rev. Ike

"Push on — keep moving!" ~ Thomas Morton

"The business of life is to go forward." ~ Samuel Johnson

"God helps them that help themselves." ~ Benjamin Franklin

AFFIRMATIVE TREATMENT

Right here and right now, I give myself a push — in the right direction!

I don't have to wait for anybody else to come along and give me a push.

I know through the Presence and Power of God within I can be what I want to be, do what I want to do, and have what I want to have!

I AM setting positive goals for myself, and giving my mind and my life a purpose.

I AM achieving and accomplishing good through the Presence and Power of God-in-me.

Thank you, Father.

Thank you, God-in-me!

REVIEW QUESTIONS

1. Whom should you look to for a push? Why?

2. How can you give yourself a push in the right direction?

3. Personal Question: Name two things that you can do to give yourself a push in the right direction.

4. What do you really want to be? What do you really want to do? What do you really want to have?

Chapter 23

THE POWER OF COMMAND

Dr. Frederick Eikerenkoetter

I and my Father are one. John 10:30

A SCIENCE OF LIVING PRINCIPLE

You are in command of the infinite God-Power within you. Decide what you want and get out of the way of the God-Power.

I get so excited when I tell you about the Power of God that is within you. If for just one split second you realized how much power you have, it would literally, in the language of the street, "blow your mind."

You Are the Power

We are all one and a part of the Infinite. This is what the Master Jesus meant when he said, *"I and my Father are one."* (John 10:30) I AM one with the Infinite. You see, it is not enough for the Infinite to just be infinite. The Infinite must define Itself through man. The Infinite must define Itself through you. The Infinite must define Itself through me. The Infinite becomes definite in man — in me, in you. The only personality that God has is in man and as man.

You have within you the potential and the power to be what you want to be, to do what you want to do, and to have what you want to have. Through *you*, the infinite Power of God becomes definite. Affirm this statement in the first person, "Through me, the infinite Power of God becomes definite."

Through man, the Infinite becomes definite, and it is your responsibility to be definite. You cannot turn away from being definite. You cannot turn away from making choices. You cannot turn away from making decisions. This is your ability and your responsibility.

Through *you*, the infinite Power of God becomes definite. It is not enough for God to be infinite; the Infinite must also be definite.

The Infinite Has Given You the Ability and the Responsibility

The Infinite has given you the ability and the responsibility to *choose* and to *define* that which you wish to be, to do, and to have. And I like to be redundant about this, because I realize many of us coming from religious backgrounds have been taught to pray to the Infinite saying, "Now Lord, you tell me what you want me to be. You tell me what you want me to do, Lord. You tell me what you want me to have, Lord." But this won't work. The Infinite is not going to speak to you from heaven and say to you, "Go thou and buy a Cadillac." The Infinite has given you the ability and the responsibility to choose the kind of car you want to have. The Infinite has given you the *ability* and the *responsibility* to *choose* the kind of life you want to live.

Command You Me

In the Scriptures, the Infinite says to the individual, *"Command you Me!"* (Isaiah 45:11) And this is where religious people get mixed up. The Infinite is saying, "You command Me. You define that which you wish me to do for you." Yet religious people say, "Now Lord, you tell me what you want me to do." And so they are at a stalemate with the Infinite. The Infinite says, "You command Me," and they say, "Now Lord, you tell me what you want me to do. You tell me whether you want me to be a lawyer or a doctor or what…"

The Infinite says to command its infinite expression. The Infinite put strength in you. You can take that strength, that power, and you can love with it or you can strike out with it.

The Infinite put emotions in your heart. You can take the power of your emotions and you can love or you can hate. You must choose what will be your experience in life.

The Infinite says to you, "YOU COMMAND ME! YOU TELL ME WHAT YOU WANT!"

A Word of Warning

When a person understands the power of his word, he is careful with it. It is just like an automobile. The automobile is a wonderful invention and there is a lot of power in it, but you have to be careful with it. An automobile has power to go up on the sidewalk and knock somebody down. It has power to take you over a cliff. Be sure to use the power of your word for only good and positive purposes.

Take Charge!

The moment you decide exactly what you want, the infinite God-Power within you goes to work to accomplish that good. So decide what you want and GET OUT OF THE WAY OF GOD-POWER! Don't let limited human thinking stand in the way wondering "how?" Don't let the human intellect stand in your way.

Your firm, definite decision COMMANDS the infinite God-Power within you to work for you according to your faith. But you must be definite. The God-Power within you awaits your decision. It is your Father's pleasure to give you health, happiness, love, success, prosperity, and money. The Bible says, *"It is your Father's good pleasure to give you the Kingdom."* (Luke 12:32)

QUOTES TO REMEMBER

"In me the infinite Power of God becomes definite."   ~ Rev. Ike

"The greatest thing in the world is to know how to be sufficient unto oneself."

~ Michel Eyquem de Montaigne

"Your greatest power is the power of choice."

~ Ralph Waldo Emerson

AFFIRMATIVE TREATMENT

In response to God's invitation, "Command you Me!" I now command the Infinite within me.

I command health year after year, from birthday to birthday.

I command happiness and love. I'm the happiest and most loving person I know. I make everyone else feel happy too, and they love me.

I command success and prosperity. Everything I touch becomes successful. I can have all the good I desire.

I now command money. Lots and lots of money is drawn into my life. I do not serve money. Money serves me for all my good purposes.

Thank you, Father!

Thank you, infinite God-Power in me!

REVIEW QUESTIONS

1. What does the Bible quotation, "Command you Me!" tell us?

2. Discuss why it is important to be definite with the Infinite. How does it affect our lives?

3. What happens if you turn away from making choices or decisions?

4. Can your human intellect ever get in the way of the good that you desire? How can you prevent this?

Chapter 24

THE TREASURE OF GOD-IN-YOU

Dr. Frederick Eikerenkoetter

In all your ways acknowledge Him, and He will direct your paths.
Proverbs 3:6

For where your treasure is, there will your heart be also.
Matthew 6:21

A SCIENCE OF LIVING PRINCIPLE

Every individual who was ever born into this world has one duty to perform, and that is to know himself, to discover his true self.

It is wonderful to recognize the Presence of God within you. It is wonderful to recognize the Presence of God, unlimited good, within each person. Every time I think about the idea that God is in me, it excites me. I don't know if it excites you, but one of the most exciting things in my life is to realize that the Presence of God is within me. Oh, that lights my fire. That puts "a tiger in my tank."

Get Excited About the Presence Of God-In-You

When I say, "You can't lose with the Stuff I use," I'm talking about the Presence of God-in-you, the Power of God-in-you, the infinite capability of God-in-you, the unlimited love of God-in-you. How can you lose with God-in-you?

I want you to reflect for a moment on the idea that God is within you. And I want you to get excited about that! I have seen people who, when they first learn that God is within, get so excited about it that they have what seem like miracles happen in their lives.

Something Wonderful Happens

I was in Washington some time ago, preaching at a fellowship meeting. Although it was raining hard outside, the place was jammed. So many people came to give me their wonderful testimonies. One which I will never forget was from a man who had seen me on television for the first time on the *Dinah Shore Show*. He said that for years he had been in and out of mental hospitals with a severe alcohol problem he just couldn't get rid of. His wife had written to me and had asked me to pray for him. When he found out that his wife was writing to me, he asked her, "Who is this man you're writing to?"

Then he saw me with Dinah Shore when I was talking about the Presence of God within. He felt something warm come over him and, from that time, he lost his taste for the alcohol that he didn't think he could do without. He has been a different man ever since. I have seen people get free from drugs, liberated in so many ways by just recognizing the Presence of God within.

Even the book of Proverbs tells us, *"In all your ways acknowledge Him, and He will direct your paths."* (Proverbs 3:6) Something infinitely marvelous happens when you recognize the Presence of God-in-you. So get excited about the fact that God is in you. Get excited about the fact that the love of God is within you, the mind of God is within you.

Mine, Refine, and Develop Your Infinite Treasures

Get excited about the fact that God has placed infinite treasures within your being. On the purely intellectual level, you couldn't possibly know all of the infinite treasures which God Almighty has placed within your being. But like the gold and the diamonds and the minerals in the earth, you must lay hold of these treasures that are within you and mine them and refine them and develop them.

Get excited about the fact that God is in you.

I will never forget a visit I made to the United Nations. There was a huge map on the wall telling about the poorest countries in the world. A statement said that in the poorest countries in the world, where the economy is at its lowest and the standard of living is sub-poverty, there are the richest deposits of minerals in the world buried deep within the earth. But people in those poor countries do not know how to *mine* and *refine* this wealth of minerals. And so they live in poverty day after day, walking on wealth, literally!

God-In-You Makes You Rich

No man is poor. I don't care what the "Cost of Living Index" says. I don't care what the unemployment figures say. No man is poor. *There are no poor people, only people who are not aware of the riches of God within.*

Deep within the heart of everyone, God has put the ability to be, to do, and to have the goodness of life, the riches of life. The truth of me, the truth of you, the truth of everyone is that, *"The Lord is my shepherd, I shall not want."* (Psalms 23:1) This is what the Master Jesus meant when he said, *"You shall know the truth and the truth shall set you free."* (John 8:32)

There are no poor people, only people who are not aware of the riches of God within.

When you know the truth that God is in you, when you know that good is in you, you are free. Unfortunately, the fact that God is in man is one of the best kept secrets in the universe. This is why I love to tell people, "God is in you." Many times when I speak to thousands and I suggest this, I see that it just shocks people.

Suggest That Only Good Is Within

Evangelists, most of the time, say to people, "You are full of the devil." When anyone suggests to people that they are full of the devil, they are going to act like the devil. This is why I teach parents, "Don't say your kids are bad! Whenever I visit a home and the little kids are jumping around, sometimes parents will say, unthinkingly, 'Oh, that is a bad child.' I say, 'That is an *active* child. That child is active and jumping around because he or she is happy and healthy. Be glad that your child is jumping around.'"

Deep within the heart of everyone, God has put the ability to be, to do, and to have the goodness of life, the riches of life.

I have always pitied these poor praying and fasting church ladies who are saved and are trying to get their husbands saved. They pray and fast and make a request in prayer meeting every night, "Pray for my husband to be saved." And then they go straight home and shake their finger in his face and say, "You old devil you." And that is why they don't get rid of the devil. They are always calling the devil. If you notice in my lectures, the devil scarcely gets an honorable mention.

People have said to me also, "Rev. Ike, why don't you preach about sin?" I'm through with sin. I've had enough of it. The heck with sin! If you concentrate on the devil and all his negative suggestions, you will draw them into your life. And I'm through with negatives.

Call Forth The God-In-You

It's like that man at my meeting In Washington. He was an alcoholic and a bum, sleeping in old abandoned cars, raising hell in his home whenever he did go home. He didn't need anybody to tell him that he was a sinner. He knew that he was a sinner. He needed somebody to pinpoint the good in him, the God-in-him. And when he heard me say that God was in him, then the God-in-him came forth.

Greet People with a Blessing

Be careful what you call out of people. Because whatever you call out of people, you are going to get it. Let us not suggest to ourselves, or to anyone else, that anything but good is within each person. Because, here again, "What you see is what you get." (Flip Wilson) What you see in other people is what you will get out of them. So when you see other people, greet them with the words that will call forth their good. Greet them with "The Presence of God-in-me blesses the Presence of God-in-you."

QUOTES TO REMEMBER

"There are no poor people, only people who are not aware of the riches of God within them."
~ Rev. Ike

"So much is a man worth as he esteems himself."
~ Francois Rabelais

"Know thyself."
~ Plutarch

AFFIRMATIVE TREATMENT

Right here and right now, I recognize, I acknowledge the Presence of God-in-me.

I am excited about the Presence of God, the presence of unlimited good in me.

I am excited about the love of God within me.

I am excited about the mind of God within me.

God has buried infinite treasures within my being.

I now mine, refine, and develop the infinite treasures within me.

I see only good, I see only God, in myself and in everyone else.

Thank you, God-in-me!

REVIEW QUESTIONS

1. What happens when you recognize the Presence of God-in-you?

2. What does Rev. Ike mean when he says there are no poor people on earth?

3. What did the Master Jesus mean when He said, "You shall know the truth and the truth shall set you free"? (John 8:32)

4. What happens when you suggest to people that they are full of the devil?

5. How can we call out the good in people?

Chapter 25

ALWAYS THE FATHER'S SON

For Father's Day

Dr. Frederick Eikerenkoetter

And you shall know the truth, and the truth shall make you free.
John 8:32

A SCIENCE OF LIVING PRINCIPLE

The truth of you is God, Infinite Good. The truth of you is perfection. You may go away from this truth in consciousness as the Prodigal Son did, but the truth of you, the Infinite Goodness of you, will not change.

There Is a Difference Between Truth And Fact

In this Ministry, when people are experiencing problems in their health, regardless of what the appearance is, I know in my heart and in my mind that the truth of that person is health. You see, in Mind Science, there is a difference between truth and fact. Read this carefully because I want you to get this! Sickness may be a fact of your experience, and I don't argue with that. But sickness is not the **truth** of you. And I want you to affirm this to yourself, "Sickness is not the truth of me. Health is the truth of me."

Here again, we are working with the principles that Jesus gave us. What did He say? "You shall know the truth, and the truth shall make you free." You have to know the truth about yourself and you have to keep affirming the truth of yourself. Because the way you see yourself is the way that you're going to experience life. "Health is the truth of me." Health — that's the truth of me!

You see, I teach people the truth about themselves. And this is how I practice healing on the individual level, by knowing the truth about myself. And even on those occasions when I've had a challenge on the physical level, I affirm, "Health is the truth of me. God-in-me is my health!" I know the truth of myself. And you know, that truth never changes.

Nothing can change the truth of me. Nothing can touch the truth of me.

Now the truth of me, the truth of you, the truth of every man is that each of us is made in the image and likeness of God, of good. You take for example the poverty idea. Do you know the truth about poverty? The truth is that there are no poor people. There are only people who do not know their riches in God. I'm going to repeat this and I want you to remember it. "There are no poor people; there are only people who do not know the truth of their riches in God." Yes, poverty is a fact. But it's not the truth. That's how I got out of poverty, by realizing that it's not the truth of me. When you know the truth, it sets you free from poverty.

To Come To God Is To Come To Yourself

Notice what happened to the Prodigal Son. He left the father's house, but he was still the father's son. What does that mean? He left the consciousness of his Divine Sonship, but the truth of him never changed. He was always the father's son. The relationship between the son and the father never changed. And even when the Prodigal Son was in the hog pen eating swill, he was still the father's son. The father still waited for him with his arms outstretched. And what does the Bible say? The Bible says, *"He came to himself."* (Luke 15:17)

To come to God is to come to yourself — that is what the theologians never understood. To come to your True Self, your Divine Self, your Spiritual Self, that's coming to a realization of the Presence of God-in-you. When the Prodigal Son came to himself, he came to the realization of who he was in God and who God was in him. As the Bible says, *"I and the Father are one."* (John 10:30)

The Lord Is My Shepherd

When he left the father's house, the Prodigal Son experienced the fact of poverty. He experienced the fact of sin. He experienced the fact of degradation. Yes, these were the facts, and I don't argue with facts. But you must know the difference between fact and truth. The Prodigal Son was experiencing the fact of poverty — but that was not the truth of him. The truth of him, the truth of me, the truth of you, the truth of **everyone** is that, *"The Lord is my shepherd, I shall not want."* (Psalms 23:1) That's the truth of me, the truth of you, the truth of everyone. And I want to repeat this again. I know it will probably shake a lot of people who are still dealing on the level of the intellect, but **there are no poor people. There are only people who do not know the riches of God within them.**

Deep within the heart of everyone, God has put the ability to be, to do, and to have the goodness of life, the riches of life.

Let me give you another example which will explain what I'm saying in another way. When I was visiting the United Nations a few years ago, I saw an exhibit concerning the so-called poor nations of the world. And beneath the maps of the so-called poor nations of the world were words to this effect: "In all of these countries there are rich minerals in the earth. But the people do not yet have the knowledge or the experience to bring out these minerals and develop them and market them." When I saw that I said to myself, "Now that's what I'm trying to say on the individual level. That's true of every man who has not yet come to know the Unlimited Resources of Good within."

God's Unlimited Goodness Is Within

The Presence of God is in every man. The Power of God is in every man. The Mind of God is in every man. The unlimited goodness of God is in every man. But man suffers because he does not know this. He does not know the truth of himself. And he does not know how to uncover these riches and develop them for his enjoyment and prosperity and for the enjoyment and prosperity of mankind as a whole. But when you know the unlimited goodness of God within, when you know this truth, it sets you free — free to develop the resources within yourself.

When you know this truth about yourself, you will be able to develop the resources that God has put within you. Acknowledge His Presence and believe in His Power. Continue to study the Mind Power techniques which I give you and work with these positive ideas every day. When you believe in yourself properly, when you accept the truth about yourself, you will know the truth of who you are in God and who God is in you. And you will know that through the Presence and Power of God within, you can be, do, and have the good that you desire.

QUOTES TO REMEMBER

"Deep within the heart of everyone, God has put the ability to be, to do, and to have the goodness of life, the riches of life."

~ Rev. Ike

"[To] learn what is true in order to do what is right, is the summing up of the whole duty of man."

~ Thomas Huxley

"There are no poor people, only people who do not know the riches of God within them."

~ Rev. Ike

AFFIRMATIVE TREATMENT

The truth of me is health.

God-in-me is my health!

The truth of me is happiness.

I AM such a happy person that everybody likes to be around me.

The truth of me is love.

I AM surrounded by love.

The truth of me is success and prosperity.

God-in-me gives me new and exciting ideas that make me successful and prosperous.

The truth of me is money.

The money-making Mind of God-in-me gives me right ideas that bring money and great things into my life.

Thank you, God-in-me!

REVIEW QUESTIONS

1. What is the difference between "a fact of your experience" and "the truth of you"?

2. What is the truth of you?

3. How does the Science of Living define "poor people"? Why?

4. What does it mean to leave the Father's house? When a person leaves the Father's house, does he leave the Father? Why or why not?

5. What are the raw materials, the resources within you? Who gave them to you? How do you develop them?

Chapter 26

PRAISE THE LORD!

Dr. Frederick Eikerenkoetter

I will bless the Lord at all times; His praise shall continually be in my mouth. Psalms 34:1

A SCIENCE OF LIVING PRINCIPLE

The more you praise the Lord, the more you will have to praise the Lord about.

Praise and Thanks Multiply Good

The more you praise the Presence of God-in-you, the more good you receive! Praise multiplies goodness. Praise multiplies blessings. And the Power of God within just loves to work for people and through people who give praise and thanks. When you give praise and you give thanks, negative thoughts can't hold you, negative conditions can't touch you.

This reminds me of a lady years ago who came to one of our Healing and Blessing Meetings on crutches. I remember that day! We were singing, rejoicing, and giving thanks. And while she was giving praise, giving thanks, giving honor to the supreme Power of God within her, she went into a different level of consciousness, dropped her crutches and was healed. I saw her the last time I was in Georgia, and she was still healed and was as healthy as can be. And I've seen that happen many, many times at our meetings across the nation. When you learn to praise the Presence of God- in-you, and you learn to thank the Presence of God-in-you for your health, healings will take place.

I'm going to suggest to you that you make praise and thanksgiving and rejoicing an everyday part of your life. You ought to wake up in the morning rejoicing and giving praise.

Rejoice In Each Day

In the Bible, the Psalmist David would wake up and he would shout, *"This is the day which the Lord hath made; I will rejoice and be glad in it!"* (Psalms 118:24) When you wake up, say to yourself — shout it to yourself if you want — "This is the day which the Lord has made; I will rejoice and be glad in it!" When you praise and rejoice in this way, negative thoughts and experiences won't come near you.

And again, we read that David shouted, "I will bless the Lord at all times; His praise shall continually be in my mouth." Everything you think should praise God. And all of your thoughts should praise God! You should not think any thought that does not praise God. For example, the thought, "I don't have any money," doesn't praise God. Whenever you say, "I can't," you are not praising God. All of your words and thoughts should praise God.

"My Cup Runs Over!"

You have to learn to give thanks for the goodness of God within. You have to learn to give thanks for the unlimited abundance of God. The more you give thanks and the more you give praise, the more you will have to give thanks and praise for. You'll get to that point like David, who kept praising God, and God just kept on blessing him and pouring out so many blessings on him until one day David just shouted, *"My cup runneth over!"* (Psalms 23:5)

You should get to that point in your prayer life that you never have to ask for anything anymore. You should get to that point in your prayer life where you, too, can think and say, "My cup runs over." Sometimes I say it like this: "I AM standing under the spout where the blessings are pouring out!" Make this praise a part of your life every day: "I AM STANDING UNDER THE SPOUT WHERE THE BLESSINGS ARE POURING OUT!"

With The Mouth, Confession Is Made

You see, you have to be careful what you say. You remember in the New Testament it says, *"With the heart, a man believes unto righteousness. And with the mouth, confession is made unto salvation."* (Romans 10:10) Most of the time, people don't get the full meaning of that. Now whatever you confess, you're going to have. If you confess the devil, you'll have him.

People just go around all day wondering why they can't be, do, and have the good they desire. And all day long, they are affirming and confessing poverty. You say, "I don't know why I can't get any money. I can't hold on to money! Money is hard to get!" You are running your rattletrap and cursing yourself every minute. You are confessing poverty, and that is what you are going to get. Again, the Book says, *"Thou art ensnared by the words of your mouth."* (Proverbs 6:2)

Find a Positive Way to Talk About a Negative Fact

I had an experience at an Atlanta college campus that I've had many times with many people. I helped a particular young lady change her words and her thoughts from negative to positive. When I first met her, she said to me, "Rev. Ike, I don't have any money." I said, "Don't say that." She said, "But Rev. Ike, that's a fact. I don't have any money and that is a fact." I told her, "Well, I don't argue with you about that being a fact. If you say it's a fact, it probably is. But it's not the truth of you. The truth of you is the prosperity, the abundance of God-in-you." Whenever there is a negative fact in your life, instead of affirming that negative fact, find a positive way to talk about that fact. Say to yourself, "God-in-me is my wealth."

Instead of saying, "I don't have any money," turn that around and say, "I see myself having all the money that I need, through the Presence and Power of God-in-me."

144

Your Happiness Praises God

Make it a habit to always say positive affirmations. When you wake up in the morning, go into words of praise the first thing. Sing happy songs while you are getting dressed, while you are getting ready to meet the day. Even if you can't carry a tune, sing anyway. If you don't know any gospel songs to sing, sing something else that's happy and positive. As long as it's happy, sing it! As long as it's positive, say it! Maybe you want to bounce around and sing. That's praise! That stirs up the joy of the Lord. You know, joy is holy. Joy in your heart always praises God. Your happiness praises God! And all of your thoughts should praise God.

QUOTES TO REMEMBER

"All of your thoughts should praise God."   ~ Rev. Ike

"Praise God, from whom all blessings flow."   ~ Bishop Thomas Ken, Morning and Evening Hymn

"I AM standing under the spout where the   ~ Rev. Ike
blessings are pouring out."

"O all ye works of the Lord, bless ye the   ~ The Song of
Lord: praise Him and exalt Him above all   the Three Holy
forever."   Children

AFFIRMATIVE TREATMENT

I give thanks to this Presence of God-in-me, this Presence of Infinite Good.

All my thoughts praise God.

I open my mind to God's blessings of health, happiness, love, success, prosperity, and money.

I AM standing under the spout where the blessings are pouring out.

Thank you, God-in-me!

REVIEW QUESTIONS

1. What happens when you praise and give thanks to the Father?

2. Can praise and rejoicing cause healing? How?

3. What should you do whenever there is a negative fact in your life?

4. What happens when you confess poverty?

5. What point should you reach in your prayer life? What does it mean to say, "My cup runneth over"?

6. What does happiness have to do with praise?

The Living God

The Living God is very true,
Because what He's done for others, He'll do for you.
And, therefore, do not accept doubt and fear,
Because God is always here.
Never be bound to anything in life but success,
And do everything with your very best.
In God's mind I AM healthy,
And casting away doubt, I AM wealthy.
And now let go of all negation,
And send Love to the other nations.
I AM the silence that is more than sound,
And within me, God is found.
God has prepared the way for us here,
And has prepared the way for us there.
I turn to that inner light
And see with my inner sight.

Tyler Morgan
age 9

Chapter 27

SPIRITUAL INDEPENDENCE

For Independence Day

Dr. Frederick Eikerenkoetter

Stand fast in the liberty with which Christ hath made us free, and be not entangled again with the yoke of bondage. Galatians 5:1

A SCIENCE OF LIVING PRINCIPLE

It is up to the individual to free himself from the negative beliefs and teachings that keep him from acknowledging his Divine Mind, that keep him from acknowledging the Presence and Power of God within. Knowing the Presence, the Power of God-in-you, will set you free — free from limitation, free to be what you want to be, to do what you want to do, and to have what you want to have.

In this Ministry we teach spiritual independence. We teach you not to depend on a god in the sky. We teach you not to depend on anybody or anything except your own Divine Self. We teach you to depend only on the Presence and Power of God within you. Through the Presence and Power of God that are within you, you can be what you want to be, you can do what you want to do, and you can have what you want to have! You will find that you don't have to wait around for somebody else to give you the good things that you want.

Many people are spiritually lazy. Many people don't **want** to be spiritually independent. They want to put their lives in the hands of somebody else or something else. They would rather depend on somebody or something else than accept responsibility for what they have or for what they don't have. They don't **want** self-responsibility! But I say to you, as long as you depend on anybody or anything else to give you the things you need, you're not free. As long as you make somebody else or something else responsible for your experience in life, you're not free — you're a slave. And that's why I don't agree with the welfare system in the U.S.A. Welfare keeps people from achieving self-responsibility. It is modern-day slavery.

The Power Within You

Each one has the power within to be independent — to be self-reliant. And what I'm saying now comes back to the one thing I'm always talking about — self-awareness. Know that the Presence of God is within you. Know that the Power of God is within you. Know the truth about who and what you are in God and who and what God is in you. Knowing this truth will set you free.

I don't teach that I have some kind of power that other people don't have. Whatever "power" you think I have, this power is also in you. But some people would have you think that they have some special privilege with God. Don't you ever believe anyone who tells you that he has some gift from God that you don't have! God does not have any favorite people. And anybody who thinks he is "holier than thou," stay away from that person! Don't associate with that kind of person!

Some people think that Jesus could do such healing work and could perform such miracles because God had given Him special powers. God didn't give Jesus anything He didn't give to you! The only difference between Jesus and you is consciousness or self-awareness. Jesus was always saying, "The Father in me, He doeth the work." (John 14:10)

Jesus was aware of His oneness with God. Jesus was aware that the Father was within Him. His knowledge of the Presence and Power of God within Him, His faith and belief in God-in-Him, was the secret of His power. This was the source of His Power.

The same Presence of God that was in Jesus is in you. The same Power of God that was in Jesus is in you.

It is the Presence and Power of God within you that you communicate with when you pray for the good you desire. It is only the God-Presence, the God-Power within you that works for you to bring about whatever good you want. That's why in this Ministry when we "pray," we point to ourselves and say, "The Presence and the Power of God are in me. The Presence and the Power of God-in-me do the work!"

A poet named Retsama wrote:

> I at last have reached the goal,
> And solved the mystery of my soul;
> I am that to which I prayed.
> That to which I looked for aid,
> I am that which I did seek,
> I am my own mountain peak.

If you are looking for a god-in-the-sky to depend on, if you are looking for a god outside of you to help you, forget it! God is within you. And when you discover God, you will discover Him within your own being.

Some people spend their entire lives praying for "God's will." People say to me, "Rev. Ike, I want to come to your services, and I'll be there Sunday, if it's the Lord's will." I tell them, "If it's your will, you'll be there." Those of you who are seeking the will of God outside of you should know this truth. **There is no will of God outside of you to impose itself on you.** There is no God outside of you that decides what your experience in life will be.

Whatever happens in your life is decided by your own state of mind. You are the one who decides whether or not you are going to be an independent, self-sufficient person. You are the one who decides whether or not you are going to be free — free to be what you want to be, to do what you want to do, and to have what you want to have.

QUOTES TO REMEMBER

"God didn't give Jesus anything He didn't give to you!"
~ Rev. Ike

"There is no will of God outside of you to impose itself on you."
~ Rev. Ike

"The somebody that you need to lean on is your Self — your Divine Self, God-in-you."
~ Rev. Ike

AFFIRMATIVE TREATMENT

Right here and right now, I accept the Presence and Power of God within that sets me free.

I AM a responsible person and have made the positive, affirmative decision to be self-sufficient and independent.

I look to the Presence and Power of God within to bring about my every good desire.

I know that the Presence and Power of God within are my Infinite Source of all good.

REVIEW QUESTIONS

1. What was the secret and source of Jesus' power?
2. What is the difference between Jesus and the average person?
3. Do you find yourself depending on someone else or something else to solve your problems or to tell you the answer?
4. If you are having a problem or challenge, to whom should you go for aid?
5. Do some people have a special privilege with God? Why or why not?
6. Who decides whether you will receive the good things in life? Why?
7. How do you become spiritually independent?

Chapter 28

BE RIGHT
BEFORE YOU UNITE!

Dr. Frederick Eikerenkoetter

And this I pray, that your love may abound more and more in knowledge and in all judgment. Philippians 1:9

A SCIENCE OF LIVING PRINCIPLE

You must be right with yourself before you can be right for someone else.

I always insist on counseling couples before they get married. And I have found that in too many cases, many people look for someone else to make them happy when they haven't found happiness within themselves. I have found that too many people look to other people for the answer to their problems, instead of looking within.

You have to get your own house in order before you can set up house with someone else.

Before an individual can unite his life with someone else, he must be financially, emotionally, and spiritually right with himself.

Romance With Finance!

So many times young women come to me and say, "Rev. Ike, my boyfriend and I want to get married." And the first thing I ask is,

"Does he have a job? Does he have any money?" Many times she'll say, "No, but we're in love." And I'll say, "You try paying the rent with that!" Between here and the pearly gates, you need some money, honey!

It's a lot easier to love and be loved when you have enough money to pay your bills and meet your needs. It's easier to love and be loved when you have enough food to eat and you don't have to worry about where your next meal is coming from. It's easier to love and be loved when you have plenty of money! Even the Bible tells us, "Money answers all things." (Ecclesiastes 10:19) Now this may be hard for some of you to take, but you know I don't preach any theological fairy tales. I don't teach you about pie in the sky by-and-by when you die. I teach that everything is better with money — even marriage. Marriage wasn't set up for you to suffer, and you won't get any reward in heaven for a bad marriage.

Romance without finance is no good.

There is a beautiful young couple who got married a few weeks ago, and I performed their wedding ceremony at United Church in New York City. When they asked me to perform their wedding ceremony, I insisted on counseling them first.

The first thing I found out was whether the husband-to-be was working. Yes, he had a job, and the woman was working, too. So, you see, one person didn't have to depend on the other financially. I counseled them and gave them some of my positive self-motivation teachings. And by the time they got married, both of these beautiful people were self-directed and self-found! They had developed a positive belief about themselves and about each other. So I agreed to perform their wedding ceremony.

Be Right with Yourself, First!

I agree with the popular song that says, "I can't be right for somebody else if I'm not right for me." And that's the way it is. When I counsel couples who are planning on marriage, I teach them that you have to be right with yourself first, you have to find yourself first, before you can go looking for someone else.

When you are right with yourself, then you will draw everyone to you who is right for you. Now the opposite is also true! If you are wrong with yourself, then you will be constantly drawing the wrong people into your life who will always be doing you wrong!

And you know, of course, it's the same way with love. You must be right with yourself and love yourself correctly first, before you can really love someone else. And I'll tell you this again — if you love yourself correctly, you will give love correctly and receive love correctly.

Find Your Own Happiness

Part of being right with yourself and loving yourself correctly is being happy with yourself. You're only going to find the happiness in other people that you, first of all, have found within your own being. If you're not happy with yourself, you're not going to be happy with anybody else, not even your husband or wife.

And you know, it's a wonderful thing to find someone and to fall in love. **But don't think that it is someone else's responsibility to make you happy! Don't give somebody else the responsibility for your happiness.** And don't blame anyone else for your misery, either. Oh no! And I'm talking to all of you who are already married, too! You have to look within yourself first and find your **own** happiness. Then you can be happy with somebody else.

Your happy feelings about yourself will go before you and bring happiness into your life.

Get A Good Start!

If you do decide to get married, be sure you get off to a good start. I've discovered that too many people get off on the wrong foot because of those old messy words that the theologians put in the wedding ceremony hundreds and hundreds of years ago.

Even today, people who are getting married are reciting these words: "I take thee to be my lawfully wedded husband (or wife), for richer or for poorer, for better or for worse, till death do us part." Well, honey, that's a jinx! Who wants to marry for poorer? Who wants to marry for worse? You can do bad by yourself! You don't need anybody to help you be **poorer**!

It's very important that you get a good start by using positive, happy, loving words in the wedding ceremony. Because the words that you speak will go forth and bring to you that which you say. The Prophet Isaiah understood this when he said, *"The word that goes forth out of my mouth; it shall not return unto me void, but it shall accomplish that which I please..."* (Isaiah 55:11)

When I perform a wedding ceremony, I don't recite that old "richer or poorer or better or worse" jive. I teach you to go into every day with an expectation of good. I teach you to believe in the Presence and Power of God within — as your Infinite Source of All Good. When you go into marriage positively, when you go into life "for richer" and "for better," this is what you will experience — the riches and the goodness of life and that more abundantly.

QUOTES TO REMEMBER

"Hasty marriage seldom proveth well."   ~ Shakespeare

"Between here and the pearly gates, you   ~ Rev. Ike
need some money, honey!"

"Of a good beginning cometh a good   ~ John Heywood
ending."

"Romance without finance is no good."   ~ Rev. Ike

AFFIRMATIVE TREATMENT

Right here and right now I resolve to love myself correctly.

I know that I must be right with myself before I can be right with someone else.

I see myself as a whole, happy, and healthy individual.

I let the Love of God-in-me radiate from me.

The Love of God-in-me draws to me all the right people for every right purpose.

Because I am right with myself, everyone and everything is compelled to be right with me.

Thank you, God-in-me!

REVIEW QUESTIONS

1. Why is financial stability important to a marriage?

2. The popular song says, "I can't be right for somebody else if I'm not right for me." Why is this true?

3. According to the Science of Living, when are you "ready" for marriage?

4. Who is responsible for your happiness? Why?

5. What is wrong with the traditional wedding vows, "for richer, for poorer, for better, for worse"? Why? How could they be rewritten in keeping with the Science of Living?

Chapter 29

I **AM** SOMEBODY!

Dr. Frederick Eikerenkoetter

With God all things are possible. Matthew 19:26

All things are possible to him that believeth. Mark 9:23

A SCIENCE OF LIVING PRINCIPLE

There is only one thing in life that nobody can take away from you. And that is the truth of you — the truth that you are a Child of God.

One of the greatest verses of Scripture that I love so much are the words of the Apostle Paul, "Be not conformed to this world, but be you transformed by the renewing of your mind." (Romans 12:2) This means do not accept things as they are if you don't like them. If you're in a poverty condition, you don't have to accept that. You don't have to conform to poverty. You don't have to conform to ignorance. You don't have to conform to sadness. You don't have to conform to depression. Be changed "by the renewing of your mind."

You change your conditions by changing your self-image.

Your conditions are not going to change until you change your self-image! And one way to change your self-image is by talking yourself up. This is why I love the slogan, "I AM somebody!" When you say to yourself, "I AM somebody!" that's talking yourself up. And if you learn how to talk yourself up, then nobody will be able to talk you down.

Lift Yourself Up!

What I am saying reminds me of another very beautiful verse of Scripture, "When men are cast down, thou shalt say, There is lifting up... "(Job 22:29) Whenever things look bad, you should say, "There is lifting up. I have the power to change my conditions by changing my mind." You should say, "I AM somebody!" And your positive belief in yourself will lift you out of any negative condition into a more positive experience in life.

You Are What You Think You Are!

If you think you're a nobody, you will be a nobody. But if you believe in yourself as a somebody, you will lift yourself up, you will BE somebody! Tell yourself that you are what you want to be. Tell yourself that you are having what you want to have, and doing what you want to do.

Don't Tell Me Your Hard Luck Story!

I remember when I was a boy working in a greasy auto repair shop back in South Carolina. And I remember the head mechanic would say to me, while I was scraping the grease off the floor, "Do you think you'll ever amount to anything?" Perhaps he meant, "Look at you, scraping up grease. You don't even have shoes to wear." And I didn't even have shoes to wear back then when I was a kid working in that little shop. I could have let that break my spirit. I could have become discouraged. But every time he asked me, "Do you think you'll ever amount to anything?" I would straighten up, stick out my chest, lift up my head and look him right in his eyes, and I'd say, "YES, Sir!"

I learned that I AM somebody and I knew it then as a kid in that greasy shop. And knowing this has brought me out of poverty into prosperity – knowing that I AM somebody brought me into a wonderful experience of success and prosperity! So don't tell me your hard luck story, because I know all about so-called "hard luck." And I know that what you believe about yourself is what determines your experience.

_____

You have to talk yourself up and tell yourself that you ARE somebody.
_____

Say to yourself, "I AM somebody!" When you know you ARE somebody, you will lift yourself up, you will rise above your negative conditions. You will be able to be what you want to be, do what you want to do, and have what you want to have. And you see, this is what you have to do with your self-image. You have to manipulate it to believe in yourself positively and correctly. When somebody asks you, "Are you going to amount to anything?" you have to straighten up and say "YES!" You have to say "Yes, I AM somebody!"

Say "YES" To Your Dreams!

Say "YES" to your dreams! Say "YES" to your good desires! Say "YES" to your lofty aspirations! Say "YES" to that vision that's in your heart! Say "YES" to that positive idea that comes to you! Say "YES" to that fire that keeps burning! Say "YES" to that wheel that keeps turning! And if you do, you'll find that they can't take that away from you. Whatever you feel about yourself, whatever you believe about yourself, must come to pass. And nobody can take that away from you! Because you ARE somebody!

QUOTES TO REMEMBER

"Things do not change; we change."   ~ Henry David Thoreau

"You must live as you think. If not, sooner or later you end up thinking as you have lived."   ~ Paul Valéry

"If you tell me how you get your feeling of importance, I'll tell you what you are. That determines your character. That is the most significant thing about you."   ~ Dale Carnegie

"Say 'YES' to your dreams!"   ~ Rev. Ike

AFFIRMATIVE TREATMENT

I AM somebody!

I AM a Child of God. I believe in myself positively and correctly.

Through the Presence and Power of God-in-me, good things are multiplying in my experience.

I AM healthy, happy, loving, successful, and prosperous.

I AM being what I want to be, doing what I want to do, and having what I want to have.

Thank you, Father!

Thank you, God-in-me!

REVIEW QUESTIONS

1. Explain how your thinking makes you a "somebody" or a "nobody."
2. How can you talk yourself up?
3. How can you get out of any negative condition?
4. What is the truth of you that nobody can take away from you?

Chapter 30

SEEING WITH THE MIND'S EYE

Dr. Frederick Eikerenkoetter

Thy Father, who sees in secret, shall reward you openly.
Matthew 6:6

A SCIENCE OF LIVING PRINCIPLE

Whatever you want, see yourself as the one who has it.

In this Ministry, in order to bring the good that you desire into your experience, we teach you to visualize. By the technique of "visualization," you can direct the attention of your mind toward the good you desire. Develop the technique of visualization. Learn to use your imagination to "see" yourself already being, doing, and having the good which you desire. Because you can be, do, and have anything that you direct your attention to, anything that you can see yourself being, doing, and having. But to bring your good desires into your experience, you must first learn how to visualize. You must first learn how to see yourself with that good which you desire.

Open Your Inner Eye

When I say that you must "see" the good you desire, I am not speaking of seeing with your physical eyes. I am speaking of seeing with your Mind's Eye, the inner eye of your imagination. That is visualization. That is where the real seeing is done. Whatever you can see yourself with in your mind, you will bring into your experience. One of the greatest Gospel truths that has ever been spoken is the phrase used by the comic Flip Wilson: "What you see is what you get!" And it's so true. You're not going to get any more in life than what you can visualize yourself with.

Whatever you can see, you can be!

It sounds simple, but there is great power in this technique. You see, you cannot receive anything unless you first can conceive the idea of it in your mind. You cannot become rich and famous if you don't first have the idea of being rich and famous. Now maybe you don't want to be famous — that's okay. It's not for everybody. But maybe you would like to take a winter vacation. Maybe that's something that you've always wanted to do but thought you'd "never get the chance."

In this lesson we're going to have a little fun, but in a serious way. We're going to learn how to apply the techniques of visualization to get a winter vacation. Now those of you who have been to my meetings already know how this is done. But for those of you who have never done this with me in person, this is how we visualize.

<u>First</u> Decide Where You Want To Go!

The first thing you must do is to decide, clearly and decisively, exactly what it is that you want. You see, many of you have never taken a winter vacation because you never made it clear in your own mind just where you wanted to go! Your mind is ready to work for you, but you have to tell it what you want it to do!

This reminds me of one of my meetings, when I was teaching about visualization. I told everybody there to get their passports ready for where they wanted to go on vacation, and get ready to travel. A few weeks later, a lady wrote to me and said, "Reverend, I have my passport, and I'm ready to travel. I don't know where I'll be going, but I'm ready to go!" Well, that lady would still be sitting in her house with her passport if I hadn't told her what I'm going to tell you now. First you have to decide exactly where you want to go, then you can visualize yourself being there. It's just like asking for directions — if you don't know where you are going, you'll never get there!

I want you to ask yourself these questions, and I want you to be very specific and very decisive when you answer.

- What kind of winter vacation do I want to go on? Where do I want to go?
- What month and day do I want to go?
- What do I want to do when I get there?
- How long do I want to stay?

Once you have clearly decided, then you can begin seeing yourself being, doing, and having that which you have chosen.

Prepare Yourself for Good

Once you have decided exactly what you want, it's important that you continually impress your subconscious with the idea of having it. Do things that will prepare you, mentally and physically, for the good that you desire. Get full of the feeling of being, doing, and having the good which you have chosen.

Begin impressing your subconscious mind with a winter vacation by going to a travel agency and getting travel brochures. Look at the beautiful pictures of the places you want to go to, and put the brochures all around your house. Impress your subconscious mind with the idea of already being there. And while you're at the travel agency, talk to the travel agent about first-class flights or boat cruises to the places you want to go.

Go shopping for the clothes you will wear while you're traveling, and look for beautiful pieces of luggage to carry your new clothes in! Find out about the famous sites you want to see while you're there, and the different, exotic foods that you want to taste. Make a list of the type of shops you want to visit, and the beautiful and expensive gifts you will buy for yourself! And if you want to travel to a foreign country, get your passport ready. Even begin learning the language of that country!

Impress your subconscious mind with the good you desire. Get full of the feeling of having new, exciting, wonderful experiences.

Once you have accepted an idea in your mind, everything necessary for the fulfillment of that idea begins to happen. Your visualization, your belief, will go before you and lead you to all the ways and means of manifesting a first-class vacation for yourself!

Now I want you to get relaxed and comfortable, and open your Mind's Eye, the inner eye of your imagination, because I want you to impress your subconscious mind with the idea of a winter vacation. Read this Vacation Visualization Prayer slowly, out loud or silently, and get "full of the feeling" of already being on your vacation. Before you go to sleep each night, reread this prayer to reinforce your subconscious mind with the idea of a vacation. And each morning when you wake up, read it again, to bring your good desires into your life.

Vacation Visualization Prayer

Here I am on the beach, enjoying the vacation of my dreams.
I wriggle my feet, and I can feel the sand between my toes.
I see myself wading into the surf, and I feel the water splashing around my ankles.
Oh, how cool it is.
I think I'll sit in the water and let it splash around me.
Ah, how relaxing this vacation is.
The sun is so warm here.
It's snowing back home.
I think I'll stay an extra day.
These people here are so nice, so friendly.

I love tasting delicious, exotic foods.

I love shopping in the beautiful little shops and buying myself lots of wonderful, expensive gifts.

This vacation is doing me a lot of good.

My bills are all paid up, and it sure is good not to have to worry about money.

I just feel so good.

Thank you, Father.

Thank you, God-in-me.

THINGS TO THINK ON

Choose a place you have always wanted to visit, and take yourself there on a Visualization Prayer Treatment. And don't forget to get an up-to-date passport! Do it today!

QUOTES TO REMEMBER

"Where there is no vision, the people perish."   ~ Proverbs 29:18

"God has given man the power to create   ~ Rev. Ike
his experience by means of his imagination;
therefore whatever he can see himself
being, doing, and having in his imagination,
he can be, do, and have in his experience."

"What you see is what you get!"   ~Flip Wilson

AFFIRMATIVE TREATMENT

God-in-me has given me the power to create my experience by means of my imagination.

I AM using my imagination to see all the good I desire in my experience.

I AM visualizing positive, happy, loving, successful experiences.

I see myself being, doing, and having all the good I desire, right here and right now.

Thank you, Father.

Thank you, God-in-me.

REVIEW QUESTIONS

1. What is visualization? How does it affect your experience?

2. Where have you decided to go on your vacation? Be specific.

3. Name all the wonderful things you will do when you go on your vacation.

Chapter 31

TREAT YOURSELF RIGHT!

Dr. Frederick Eikerenkoetter

Whosoever hath, to him shall be given, and he shall have more abundance; but whosoever hath not, from him shall be taken away even what he hath. Matthew 13:12

A SCIENCE OF LIVING PRINCIPLE

You are the most important person in your life.

I want to ask you a question. Who is the most important person in your life? Think about that carefully.

Too many people have been brought up to believe that they are not important, that they should put themselves last. I heard somebody say the other day, "I'm third. God is first, other people are second, and I'm third." But I disagree with that. Who is the most important person in your life? **You** are the most important person in your life.

Put Yourself First

Now that might sound egotistical, so let me explain. When I say to you that you are number one, when I say that you are the most important person in your life, I don't mean that other people aren't important. I don't mean that you shouldn't have lots of good friends. I mean that what you think of yourself determines what other people think of you. You have to learn to treat yourself right before you can treat other people right, and before other people will treat you right. You have to believe that you are number one.

This reminds me of a well-known car rental company that says, "We're not number one, we're only number two, but we're trying." Well, you know what happens? Everyone who hears that goes to the number one company for their business! If you don't believe you're number one, if you don't believe that you're the best, nobody else will!

Be Your Own Best Friend

A lady once said to me, "Rev. Ike, I don't know why, but my children don't treat me right. I do everything for them. I spend all my money on them. Even if I need something, I give it to them first." Well, I'll tell you just what I told that lady: "Those children are treating you the same way you are treating yourself! By denying yourself, you are telling them, 'I don't matter, I'm not important.' "

___

The way you treat yourself tells other people how to treat you.

___

You have to treat yourself correctly. You have to "be your own best friend." Because if you don't treat yourself correctly, then how can you expect others to treat you correctly? If you are having trouble with someone, if someone is treating you as an enemy instead of as a friend, look within to see how **you** are treating **you**!

When you treat yourself correctly, you will treat everyone else correctly. And everyone will be compelled to treat you correctly.

Be Good To Yourself!

You are the most important person in your life — so be good to yourself! Be nice to yourself! Treat yourself to something that you always wanted. It doesn't have to be an expensive gift. Treat yourself to something that you've always wanted but never bought because you didn't think you deserved it.

Enjoy the Good You Have

Some people don't know how to be good to themselves. Some of you don't even enjoy the good things that you already have. Some of you even have furniture that you think is too good for you to sit on! So you save it for company. Well, honey, you are your own best company! Some of you have your good linen and silverware packed away in a trunk, and you're saving it till the preacher comes to dinner. You think it's good enough for the preacher but it's not good enough for you! Well, I'll tell you this, when you can't enjoy the good that you have, this deprives you of having more good. **Because the more you enjoy the good you have, the more good you will have to enjoy.**

The old spiritual had the right idea, "Everyday's gonna be Sunday!" Be good to yourself, and make every day Sunday!

The enjoyment of good increases and multiplies the good.

I'll never forget how my dear mother, for years and years, kept her best things and her nicest things packed in a big, old trunk. And maybe three times a year she'd go through that trunk. And oh! I used to love to be around then. She would open that trunk, and it smelled so good, you know, with the sachet powder... she even had gifts in there that old friends had given her long ago — precious perfumes, precious linens. And she wouldn't use them. Until the day she died, she kept those things in that trunk, and never did enjoy them.

Sweeten the Now and Now!

Never think that anything is too good for you. Because there is nothing that is too good for you! Stop saving your best things and your nicest things in closets and trunks. Stop denying yourself the enjoyment of life, because you think it will please God. God wants you to enjoy life! God's goodness is meant for you to enjoy, right here and right now! So use the best and enjoy the best you have NOW! As the song says, "I'm gonna shout while I'm here!" I'm gonna sing while I'm here! I'm gonna have steak while I'm here! I'm going to have filet mignon and Chateaubriand while I'm here! I'm going to enjoy the sweet now and now!

The best way to prepare for the sweet by-and-by is to sweeten the now and now!

If you don't prepare yourself for the sweet by-and-by, if you don't treat yourself right, when you finally get there, everything will be too rich for you! All your saving and denying won't do you any good then! You won't be able to enjoy it! Remember: The best way to prepare for the sweet by-and-by is to sweeten the now and now! Enjoy your good right here and right now! Treat yourself right!

.

QUOTES TO REMEMBER

"I have come that they might have life, and that they might have it more abundantly." ~ John 10:10

"There are two things to aim at in life: First, to get what you want; and after that, to enjoy it..." ~ Logan Pearsall Smith

"Love yourself and your own affairs without any rival." ~ Horace

"The enjoyment of good increases and multiplies the good." ~ Rev. Ike

AFFIRMATIVE TREATMENT

I AM the most important person in my life.

I AM treating myself correctly.

I AM enjoying all the good I have, right here and right now.

I AM enjoying the sweet now and now.

I AM enjoying all the blessings God has bestowed upon me.

My right belief about myself goes forth and causes everyone in my experience to be right with me.

Thank you, Father.

Thank you, God-in-me!

REVIEW QUESTIONS

1. What does this lesson teach you?

2. Who is the most important person in your life?

3. Read the quote by Horace in the "Quotes to Remember" section. What does it mean?

4. Write down three examples, other than those mentioned in this lesson, of ways you can begin to enjoy more of the good you already have.

Chapter 32

THE POWER OF FASCINATION

Dr. Frederick Eikerenkoetter

As a man thinks, so is he. Proverbs 23:7

A SCIENCE OF LIVING PRINCIPLE

God-in-you has given you the power of fascination to use to be, do, and have all the good you desire. It is up to you to determine how you will use it.

I want to tell you about the power of fascination. But first I want to give you a definition of the word "fascination." "Fascination" is an intense interest or enchantment with an idea, person, or thing. Fascination means getting tuned in and turned on to every detail of the object of your fascination. And fascination has power!

How Fascination Works

Now this may sound strange, but it's true. There **is** power in fascination. It has power because whatever you're fascinated with, you become. You automatically draw that which you are fascinated with unto you. Be it good or evil, **whatever** you are fascinated with will come into your experience.

The power of fascination has always been with us. The story is told about a young prince who was a hunchback. So his father, the king, had a statue built that looked exactly like the young, hunchbacked prince in every detail, except one. The statue was not a hunchback, but rather the statue stood erect. And so the king had this perfect, erect statue placed in the garden where the young prince would see it, as he played every day. The young prince was fascinated with the statue and looked at it every day. And this perfect, erect image of himself was impressed on his subconscious mind. Slowly, without his even being aware of it, the young prince's back began to straighten, until at last, he was no longer a hunchback. He stood tall, erect — in the exact image of the statue his father had built. He became that which he had directed his attention to each and every day.

You see how fascination works. You see how powerful fascination is. Whatever the object of your fascination is, it will be magnetized to you. When you concentrate and focus your attention on an object or idea, your mind gives power to that object or idea. Truly, it has been said, "Where your attention goes, the power flows." Whatever thoughts and ideas your mind power focuses on will manifest in your life.

Controlling the Power of Fascination

People use the power of fascination in many ways. Some people use the power of fascination negatively without even knowing it. It is important that you learn to control and direct your fascination, because of its power. When you learn to direct your mental powers, when you learn to control your power of fascination, you can control all of your experiences. This is what the Bible means when it says, "Keep thy heart with all diligence, for out of it are the issues of life." (Proverbs 4:23)

You must be careful not to use your power of fascination negatively, because it will bring negatives into your life. I want you to ask yourself some questions so that you can determine if you are using your power of fascination negatively.

When you see an accident on the highway, do you slow down and look to see how much blood there is? Do you turn to read the obituaries when you read the newspaper? Do you pick out all the worst things you can find in the paper and say, "Oh, isn't that terrible? Oh my goodness, isn't that awful?" Are you the first in line for the scariest, most morbid movie in town?

If you answered "yes" to these questions, then you are using your power of fascination negatively. If you're fascinated by horror movies, if you're fascinated by morbid stories and frightening events, it's a matter of pure Mind Science that you're going to magnetize some of this horror to yourself! You must begin to use the power of fascination positively.

The answer is within you, within the Presence of God-in-you.

Some people are fascinated with problems. They become enchanted by their problems. They give so much attention and power to their problems that they can't see anything but the problem. They even **enjoy** having problems! And because they are fascinated with their problems, they can't see the answer. The answer is already within you, but if you become fascinated with the problem instead of the answer, the answer can't come to you!

Be Fascinated With Positives!

Sometimes people become so fascinated by what they don't have, by the good they are lacking, that they can't see the good they do have. Become fascinated by the Presence of God, Infinite Good, that is within you. Become fascinated by the Power of God that is within you to achieve the good that you want to achieve. If you want to be a healthy person, become **fascinated** with health! Become **intensely interested** in the idea of health! Become enchanted with the idea of health! If you want to be successful, become fascinated with success! Become intensely interested in success and successful people!

You people who have not yet decided what you want to be, do, and have in life, think of the good you want, and become fascinated with the idea of being, doing, and having it. If you want to become a doctor, get fascinated with the idea. Look for a job in a doctor's office. Associate with people in the medical profession. Study up on how to become a doctor.

This reminds me of a man I met a few months ago in California who is in his early thirties and is the owner of a large automobile dealership. He told me, "I first got a job here when I was a teenager. I even hiked my age up to get the job. I was fascinated with the idea of selling automobiles, and I was fascinated with the idea of having my own automobile dealership. So I started here scraping up the grease, and sweeping up the dirt, but while I was doing that I watched the mechanics working and I watched the people in the offices. I watched the boss as he moved about the company."

Through the years that man rose in the ranks of the company. And when the owner retired, he sold the company to him. That man was fascinated with success and he became a success!

The same way that he manifested the good he desired, you can too. Whatever good you want in your experience, get **fascinated** with it! Get fascinated with the riches of life — health, happiness, love, success, prosperity, and money! Get fascinated with being the good you want to be, doing the good you want to do, and having the good you want to have, and your power of fascination will magnetize that good to you, and bring it into your experience.

QUOTES TO REMEMBER

"Mere enthusiasm is the all in all."   ~ William Blake

"There is power in fascination to bring the   ~ Rev. Ike
good you want into your life."

AFFIRMATIVE TREATMENT

Right here and right now I decide to use my power of fascination positively.

I AM fascinated with success!

I AM fascinated with prosperity!

I AM fascinated with love!

I AM fascinated with happiness!

I AM fascinated with health!

My positive powerful fascination for these good things multiplies good things in my experience.

Thank you, Father!

Thank you, God-in-me!

REVIEW QUESTIONS

1. How is fascination powerful?

2. How do you use your power of fascination? Do you use it positively or negatively?

3. What happens when you become fascinated with morbid, frightening things?

4. What good do you want in your life? How can you begin getting fascinated with it?

Chapter 33

FEED YOUR MIND RIGHT IDEAS

Dr. Frederick Eikerenkoetter

Man shall not live by bread alone, but by every word that proceeds out of the mouth of God. Deuteronomy 8:3

A SCIENCE OF LIVING PRINCIPLE

Your subconscious mind accepts whatever ideas you feed it and brings them into your experience.

Nutritionist Adelle Davis is famous for the statement, "You are what you eat." I would like to revise this statement in the Science of Living philosophy, and state that you are whatever you feed your mind. Many people don't realize that everything in your life is a reflection of the ideas, thoughts, and beliefs in your mind. It follows that you have to watch what you let your mind feed upon.

Whatever idea you feed your conscious mind with, your subconscious mind will bring it into your experience. Now that's very important, and I want you to remember that. **Whatever idea you feed your mind with, your subconscious mind will bring it into your experience.** If you feed your mind negative ideas, you're going to have negative results in your experience.

This reminds me of the way some people treat their dogs. Now this may be a bit coarse for some of you, but I've seen some people neglect to feed their dogs properly at home, and after awhile the dog leaves. And where is the dog? He's outside running around, eating anything he can find in a garbage can. You see, if the dog isn't being fed properly, he will eat what he shouldn't. And the dog ends up sick and mangy because he doesn't have the proper diet and care.

It's the same thing with your mind. If you do not consciously and regularly feed your mind positive ideas, then your mind will become just like that neglected dog and feed on the garbage of the world-mind. And you know what will come into your life? Garbage!

Feed Your Mind Properly

What should you feed your mind? You should constantly feed your mind right ideas! The Bible tells us, "Man shall not live by bread alone, but by every word that proceeds out of the mouth of God." The mouth of God is the mouth of good. The mouth of God speaks only good, positive, loving words of health, happiness, love, success, and prosperity. **This** is the spiritual and mental nutrition that your mind needs in order to manifest positives in your experience.

Your subconscious mind accepts whatever ideas you feed it and brings them into your experience.

Just as your physical body reflects health and strength when you feed it correctly, so will your life reflect the right ideas you feed your mind. But this right thinking can't be something you do only once in a while, and expect to get right results. Just like you can't eat good food once a month and expect to be healthy, you can't just think one positive thought once a month and expect your life to change for the better. **You must continually and constantly feed your mind only good thoughts, positive thoughts.** You must feast upon the idea of health. Feast upon the idea of happiness, of love, of success, and of prosperity. Stuff your mind with positive ideas. Digest all the positive teachings I give you until they become a part of you. And exercise your mind daily by practicing mental techniques of positive thinking.

Techniques for Every Day

Every day, affirm to yourself, "God-in-me is my Unlimited Source of All Good." Begin each morning with a good mental and spiritual breakfast, including positive affirmations like, "This is the day which the Lord hath made, I shall rejoice and be glad in it." (Psalms 118:24) You don't even have to get out of bed in the morning to start thinking positively — have breakfast in bed!

Lunch on ideas of health. Snack on positive beliefs and attitudes. Never let your mind go hungry for positive thoughts and positive ideas. Never let your mind starve for ideas of health, happiness, love, success, and prosperity. Always include as part of your daily diet thoughts like, "The Presence of God-in-me heals me and keeps me well." Each night before you go to sleep, have a balanced meal of good ideas.

As you feast on these positive ideas, as you practice consistent and continual positive thinking, these positive ideas will just seep into your subconscious mind. Your subconscious mind will digest these positive ideas from the Mind of God-in-you, and prepare you to experience the good you desire.

QUOTES TO REMEMBER

"Feed your mind right ideas, and your mind will lead you to the ways and means of manifesting those good ideas in your experience."

~ Rev. Ike

"Man shall not live by bread alone...."

~ Deuteronomy 8:3

"You are what you eat!"

~ Adelle Davis

AFFIRMATIVE TREATMENT

I now feed my mind with the idea of Health. I mentally and spiritually feast upon the idea of health. I feed upon the idea that God-in-me is my health. And this Divine Idea keeps me healthy!

I now feed my mind with the idea of Happiness. I turn to the Presence and Power of God within me, and I AM full of the idea of happiness. My happiness is overflowing as I spread it around.

I now feed my mind with the idea of Love. God-in-me loves me. The Love of God operating through me draws all of the right people into my experience for every right purpose. I AM enjoying the love, friendship, companionship, and romance of life.

I now feed my mind with the idea of Success and Prosperity. The Presence and Power of God-in-me give me every reason to be successful! I AM continually being led and guided into new feasts of success and prosperity!

I now feed my mind with the correct idea of Money. The correct Money-Idea in my mind draws money to me in new, exciting ways. I AM enjoying lots and lots of money in right order.

Thank you, Father!

Thank you, God-in-me!

REVIEW QUESTIONS

1. How does the food that you feed your mind and body affect you?
2. What kind of food should you feed your mind? What kind do you feed it now?
3. What is the "garbage of the world-mind"?
4. What does this mean: "You are what you feed your mind"?
5. How often should you feed your mind? Why?

Chapter 34

FOUR STEPS TO GET WHAT YOU WANT

Dr. Frederick Eikerenkoetter

Where there is no vision, the people perish. Proverbs 29:18

A SCIENCE OF LIVING PRINCIPLE

You have within you the Infinite Power of God to bring into existence whatever good you want to be, to do, and to have!

In this lesson I have outlined four steps to help you to bring the good you want into existence. Study and meditate upon **each and every step, each and every day.** They are to be studied over and over, not just read once and forgotten. These steps must become a part of you. As you discipline and condition your mind in this way, the good which you desire will come to you in ways that are *"past finding out."* (Romans 11:33)

1. **DECIDE IT!**
2. **BELIEVE IT!**
3. **SEE IT!**
4. **FEEL IT!**

Decide it — Your decision defines what you want.
Believe it — Belief is mental acceptance; mentally accept it NOW.
See it — In your mind.
Feel it — In your heart.

❶ DECIDE IT!

First **decide what it is that you want.** A very simple question to ask yourself every day is this one: "What do I want?" Write that down on a piece of paper and put that on your mirror so that every morning as you prepare for the day you can ask yourself, "What do I want?"

Although that is a simple question, many, many people have never answered it for themselves. Many people can't decide what it is they want. And many others believe that no matter what they want, they can't have it. So this holds them back from getting what they want. Now I'm telling you to leave all those thoughts of "I can't" behind! Tell yourself you **can** be, you **can** do, you **can** have what you want.

Sometimes I find it is necessary to shock people into making a decision. When people come to me and they're undecided in their minds, oftentimes I'll say to them, "What in the hell do you want?" See, they don't expect to hear a minister cuss. Some people will be so shocked, they'll blurt out, "I really don't know," Well, how in the world are you going to get something if you haven't decided what it is that you want?

Right here and right now, make up your mind about what you want and write it down. For the purposes of this lesson, let's say that your goal is to have your own business. Write down what type of business you want and write down the date when you will start your business. Make plans for the grand opening. Decide on the part of town you will have your office in. What type of building do you want your office in? Write that down. How many employees will you have? Write that down too.

If you don't want your own business, decide in your mind exactly what you do want and write that down. Maybe you want a new house, a vacation, or more education. Whatever it is, decide what your goals are **NOW** and write them down so you can have them before you as a daily reminder.

❷ BELIEVE IT!

Belief is mental acceptance. When you believe something, you mentally accept it for yourself. In order to accomplish your goals and achieve your good purposes, you have to **believe**, you have to mentally accept what you want. Do not be discouraged by those around you who tell you that you cannot accomplish your goals. Remember that the world is full of wonders that people said couldn't be done.

Believe in the Infinite Goodness, the Infinite **Power** of God-in-you. When you believe, you can achieve any and every goal you set for yourself. As Rev. Ike says, "When you believe in yourself you become UNSTOPPABLE!"

Many people write to me and tell me, "Rev. Ike, I want more for myself but I don't have enough education to accomplish my goals." I remind them that a lot of millionaires, even some **BILLIONAIRES** didn't have much education and that didn't hold them back. Many people use the lack of education as an excuse. I always encourage you to get all of the education you can, and if you are self-motivated, you'll find scholarships and grants for your education. But don't let the lack of a formal education hold you back. If you want something greatly enough, you will find a way.

❸ SEE IT!

Use the technique of visualization. You must see the goals you have set for yourself. Use your imagination to see your dreams and lofty aspirations. As Flip Wilson says so well, "What you SEE is what you get!" Go into the theater of your mind and see yourself walking into your new office to take charge. See yourself as the boss behind your desk. Visualize the carpeting on the floor — notice how thick it is? Visualize the windows and the wonderful view of the city. **See** the comfortable chairs, and picture yourself holding a conference with other business executives. Visualize your bank account bulging with lots and lots of money!

Whatever business you want, see yourself in the process of making a sale. See yourself ringing up all that money on your cash register. Whatever business you want, see yourself experiencing it. If you want something other than a business, see yourself with it. See yourself being, doing, and having the good you desire.

"Where there is no vision, the people perish."

---

❹ FEEL IT!

Feel the Presence and Power of God already within you! Feel this Power within you bringing your good purposes into reality.

See what you want and **feel** yourself experiencing it. If you're going to be a boss, see yourself behind that big boss's desk, and feel the arms of your chair. Feel the buttons on your telephone that connect you to all of your employees. Feel yourself walking on the thick colorful carpeting. Smell the new office smell. Smell the fresh flowers on your desk. Feel the plush drapes on your windows and feel the money pouring into the bank!

Feel your good purposes in your heart. And of course "seeing" and "feeling" in the subjective depth of your being go together. "See" what you want and "feel" yourself experiencing it. For example, one of the favorite techniques I teach for getting the car you want is to mentally sit in that new car and smell the new car smell. Get full of the feeling of sitting in the driver's seat and feel the notches behind the steering wheel. Feel yourself driving that car down the street.

Feel the good you desire in your heart and open the eye of your mind, the theater of your mind, to the Presence and Power of God within you. The Infinite Source of Good will bring the good you desire into manifestation. Your positive thinking and feeling will lead you to take the right positive action to accomplish your good desires.

It Cannot Be Otherwise

Too many times people want to put the responsibility for their decisions on somebody else — even somebody way up in the sky. But the important teaching here is that **you** have to decide it, **you** have to believe it, **you** have to see it, and **you** have to feel it.

In this Ministry, we not only give you theories, but we show you how to work with them. We give you practical applications. What I give to you, I know it works because it works for me. That's why I can make the extravagant claim, "You Can't Lose With The Stuff I Use!"

Study these teachings and practice these instructions, correctly and in faith, every day. As you decide, believe, see, and feel the good you desire in your heart and mind, you will receive guidance as to what you should do, from the God-Mind within you.

THINGS TO THINK ON

DECIDE, BELIEVE, SEE, and FEEL the things that you want to be, to do, and to have. Open your mind to the guidance of the Divine Mind. It will direct you what to **DO**. Co-operate with God-in-you. "And He shall bring it to pass."

QUOTES TO REMEMBER

"Climb high, climb far, your goal the sky, your aim the star."	~ Anonymous
"Every day, in every way, I'm getting better and better."	~ Émile Coué
"Again, men in general desire the good, and not merely what their fathers had."	~ Aristotle
"Positive thinking leads to positive action and positive results. Any kind of thinking that does not lead to positive action and positive results is not positive thinking."	~ Rev. Ike

AFFIRMATIVE TREATMENT

Right here and right now, I KNOW exactly what I want!

I have DECIDED it in my heart and in my mind.

I BELIEVE in the good which I desire.

I SEE and FEEL myself being what I want to be, doing what I want to do, and having what I want to have.

My positive thinking leads me to positive action. And I get positive results.

Thank you, God-in-me!

REVIEW QUESTIONS

1. How can you get what you want?

2. How often should you remind yourself of the four steps to accomplish your good purpose?

3. Where do the power and guidance to achieve your goals come from?

4. Why are these four steps to get what you want important?

5. What is the relationship between positive thinking and positive action?

MASTERY

"I, at last, have reached the Goal,
And solved the mystery of my Soul;
I am that to which I prayed,
That to which I looked for aid;
I am that which I did seek,
I am my own mountain peak;

I upon creation look
As a leaf in my own book;
For I, THE ONE, "the many" make
Of substance which from me I take;
For all is me, there are no two;
Creation is myself, all through;

What I grant unto myself,
I take down from my own shelf,
And give to me – THE ONLY ONE –
For I'M the Father and the Son.
When I want, I do but see,
My wishes coming forth in me;

For I'm the Knower, and the Known,
Ruler, Subject, and The Throne;
The "Three in One" is what I am,
Hell itself is but my dam,
Which I did put in my own stream,
When in a nightmare I did dream
"That I was not, THE ONLY ONE,"

Thus by me was pain begun,
Which ran its course till I awoke,
And found that I with me did joke,
So now that I do stand awake,
I, my throne, do wisely take,
And rule my kingdom, which is me,
A Master through Eternity."

Retsama

186

Chapter 35

THE GENEROSITY OF GOD

Dr. Frederick Eikerenkoetter

He is able to do exceedingly abundantly above all that we ask or think, according to His power that works in us. Ephesians 3:20

A SCIENCE OF LIVING PRINCIPLE

God has ordained perfect good, an abundance of good, for you — for each and every one of us. When you know that God is a God of generosity and abundance, you will experience an abundance of good in your life.

What Kind Of God Are You Praying To?

I want you to ask yourself a question. What kind of God are you praying to? If you are praying to a God to whom you have to beg and plead and kneel, you're praying to the wrong one! Sometimes I wonder how people could have such a stingy God. Because the Infinite God is really generous. The Lord is really kind and loving and wants you to have the riches of life in abundance!

When we think of God as mean, stingy, and limited, we are limiting our own happiness, our own enjoyment of life. It's just like a beggar on the street. If he only asks for a nickel, that is all he will get. He is limiting his own good. If you pray, "Ple-e-e-z-e Lord, just give me a little bit," that is exactly what you're going to get — just a little bit. That's like going to the ocean to take out water with a thimble! Why should you do that? You have to remember that you are dealing with the Infinite — the **Unlimited** Source of ALL GOOD.

The 23rd Psalm, 5th verse, bespeaks the generosity of the Lord where it reads, "My cup runneth over!" Now that's who I deal with! I deal with the Lord who runs my cup over! I deal with the concept of God in the 23rd Psalm, "The Lord is my shepherd, I shall not want." Because that's who the Lord is. "The Lord is my shepherd." And because He is, "I shall not want." The heck with that God I used to serve. Boy, was He a stingy fellow!

I want you to read this verse of Scripture:

> *"He is able to do exceedingly abundantly above all that we ask or think, according to His power that works in us."*

And what does this verse tell us? It tells us that the Lord is generous! Now, that may shock some of you saints, but that's exactly what I want to do. Some people have to be shocked out of their old ways to renew their thinking and renew their lives.

The Lord is not stingy, hard-hearted, or limited. It's man that has misused his mind to create a false, stingy, hard-hearted, hard-of-hearing God-in-the-sky. So many people today have that image of God. They still keep praying, "Oh, Lord, just give me this one little thing, and I won't ask for anything more. Just this one little thing." What nonsense!

Through the Presence of God-in-you, you can have an abundance of all the riches of life.

The Bible tells us that one time there were several thousand people out in the desert, listening to Jesus preach all day. The time came when they needed food, but the disciples could only find a little fish and bread. So they said to Jesus, "There's only a little fish and bread, and it is not enough to feed this great multitude." But the Mastermind Jesus said, "Bring it to me." He took it in His hand, lifted up His faith and said, "Thank you Father." Then Jesus said, "Now pass this out, and give them to eat." They passed it out and there was more than enough. There were several baskets of food left over after all had eaten. So you see, God **always** gives a surplus!

Abundance in Nature

Here again, I want to give you another example of the generosity of God. Every time you grow something or see a garden, you are seeing the generosity of the Lord. When you plant a seed — when it comes forth, it is very generous. On one stalk of corn, you will find several ears of corn, right? And that one stalk laden with corn in turn produces several hundred other grains of corn. You see how generous God is?

In your mind and in your prayers you must **know** that you are dealing with the generosity of the Lord. The Lord says, *"I have come that they might have life, and that they might have it more abundantly."* (John 10:10)

It has been truly said: "Anyone can count the seeds in an apple. But only God can count the apples in a seed."

You Receive What You Conceive

You can only receive what your mind can conceive. So it's very important that you establish in your mind a generous concept of God, a loving, infinite concept of God. And establish in your mind that He wants you to have and enjoy all the good you desire. Because the belief that you have in your mind is always multiplied back to you in your experiences.

When you believe that God is stingy and mean, this is what you will bring into your life. But when you reach the level of awareness that you can accept a good, loving, generous God, then your experiences in life will be abundant. When you believe that the Presence of God within is your Infinite Source of all good, you will receive an abundance of all the riches of life, of all the good you desire!

QUOTES TO REMEMBER

"God is not withholding, man is not beholding."   ~ Anonymous

"I have come that they might have life, and that they might have it more abundantly."   ~ John 10:10

"God has ordained a perfect good for you."   ~ Rev. Ike

"Ask, and it shall be given."   ~ Matthew 7:7

AFFIRMATIVE TREATMENT

God-in-me is generous in all things!

I have an abundance of health which overflows and becomes a Healing Power to everyone and everything that are a part of my consciousness.

I have an abundance of happiness which flows out of me and uplifts me and others.

I have an abundance of love. My life is a great romance, because whatever good I desire, I attract it to me. I AM in love with life.

I have an abundance of success and prosperity which moves me from glory to glory!

Through the Presence of God-in-me, I AM experiencing an abundance of all good.

My cup runneth over!

Thank you, God-in-me!

REVIEW QUESTIONS

1. How does the story about Jesus feeding the multitude show the generosity of God?

2. What should you believe about God in order to experience abundance?

3. What is meant by the quotation: "Anyone can count the seeds in an apple. But only God can count the apples in a seed"?

4. Give other examples of the generosity of God in Nature.

Chapter 36

HOW TO GET THE JOB YOU WANT

For Labor Day

Dr. Frederick Eikerenkoetter

I have spoken it, I will also bring it to pass; I have purposed it, I will also do it. Isaiah 46:11

A SCIENCE OF LIVING PRINCIPLE

Believe in yourself positively and correctly. Be positive-minded and know that you can choose to be anything you want to be, do anything you want to do, and have anything you want to have. Know that through the Presence and Power of God-in-you, your opportunities are unlimited. Believe that once you acknowledge the Infinite God within you, your experience of good will be infinite.

I'm going to teach you how to get any job or position you want. Now, I know that you've heard people say, "there just aren't any jobs," or how "everybody is unemployed." Well, that's just the kind of negative thinking that keeps people unemployed. The more the newspapers and the other media speak about unemployment, the more people catch the unemployment idea and become unemployed. They begin to panic and are defeated before they even start looking for a job, because they don't think there are any jobs. But if you think positively and believe in yourself, you will find the job you want, and it will be the right job for you.

Decide That You Are Going to Get a Job

If you want a job, you first have to sit down and decide if you want to work. Ask yourself, "Do I really want to work?" Be honest with yourself and be sure that you really **do want** to work. Be sure that you really don't want to be on unemployment compensation or welfare. Because once you get that job, you're going to have to work at it in order to keep it. Once you get a job, you can't have a complaining attitude about work. If you do, your poor work attitude will cause you to lose that job. **Be positive that you not only want to be employed, but that you also want to work.**

The next step is to decide that you are going to get a job. Trust in the Presence and Power of God-in-you that you will find the right job for you.

Be Choosy!

After you decide that you are going to get a job, sit down and decide exactly what kind of a job you want. And be choosy! It is important to be choosy about everything! Utilize the power of decision that is within you to decide and choose what you want to be, to do, and to have. Decide on a specific type of job. Aim for something better than you've ever had before, and visualize yourself in that job. Be positive about your getting the job you've decided on, and see yourself working at it. See yourself in that job. Be careful to be VERY choosy, because there must be a million kinds of jobs, and you don't want just any job. If you're not specific, you may get a job, but it won't be the "right" one for you, because you've let the world-mind choose for you instead of making the choice yourself.

Whatever you decide to do — whether it's working for a large company or starting your own business, believe that the God-Mind in you will guide you. And you must COOPERATE with God.

The moment you accept an idea, everything necessary for the fulfillment of that idea begins to happen.

Take Positive Steps

Once you have decided on the kind of job you want, you must take positive action and go after that job. I would like to learn ballroom dancing, and I'd like to learn to play the piano. But it's not enough for me to sit down and dream about what I would like to do. I must take decisive action. You must take action on the good you desire. Visualizing yourself doing what you want to do is only the **first** step. Here are some other positive steps that will help you get the job you want!

Get up and go after the job you want. Sift through the newspapers, and look in the want ads every day. Contact the best employment agencies and companies that offer the kind of job you want. Show them that you know exactly what you want. Remember that many jobs aren't even advertised. Often a positive self-starter will show a company that it needs HIM even before the company knows it.

The Résumé

Some positions require a résumé, or a summary of your talents and abilities. If the position you are applying for requires a résumé, get some books that direct you in writing one. To help you get your thoughts organized, first make a list of how and why you are qualified for the job. Think about how you can benefit an employer, and what good, positive assets you can bring to the enterprise. Your résumé should reflect a positive self-image. Reaffirm your positive self-image and build yourself up in your own mind.

No one ever got a job by merely submitting a résumé, but your résumé may be the first contact your potential employer will have with you. It is going to represent you to the person in charge. So make sure it is well written and typed accurately on quality paper. Include in your résumé all your talents and experiences that give a positive picture of you. Don't be held back by negative thinking like, "I don't have enough education," or "I don't qualify for the job." Think positively about yourself and think positively about the job you want. Think about why you want it, how you're qualified for it, and why you know you'll be happy with it.

Send out your résumé to as many companies and agencies that you can find that offer the kind of job you are looking for. Make sure you send your résumé with a neat well-written cover letter that explains who you are and why you are applying for this job.

The Job Interview

When you are called on a job interview, take some positive steps ahead of time to make sure you make a good impression. Prepare for the interview by talking to your friends as if they are the interviewers. Make sure you find out everything you can about the company before the interview, so you can show the person that you are aware of the company and interested in it. Practice speaking about yourself and how you will fit into the job. Study your list of why and how you are qualified for the job. Prepare a history of your experience, and write down in a positive way how you are prepared for the job. As Rev. Ike always says, "You can only acquire that which you can cultivate the feeling of having." So become full of the feeling of having the job you want, and you will get it!

Make a Positive Impression

It has been truly said, "You'll get where you're going a lot faster if you look like you're already there." So, look, dress, feel, and think as if you're the right person for the job! Believe that you already have the job. Your positive self-belief will create a positive impression of you. When you talk to the interviewer, look him right in the eye, and let him know you belong there. Let the Presence of God-in-you shout out the message that you are ready and right for this job. If you do this, the person interviewing you will receive your positive vibrations and consider you more favorably for the job.

Never underestimate the power of the impression you make on other people! It tells them what you think of yourself.

Believe in yourself first, and others will believe in you.

If you go to an interview looking bad, like you don't think highly of yourself — that's just the negative vibration you're going to give the interviewer. You're going to impress the person with the idea that you don't think much of yourself, and that you probably couldn't handle the job. The interviewer will count you out of the job because you've already counted yourself out! The person will respond to your negative self-image by throwing your application away!

After you have had a successful interview, go home and review in your mind all the positive ways you were able to respond to the interview. Write a brief "thank you letter" to the interviewer and include all those points that were most positive during the interview. Remind the interviewer of your best qualities, and add others that you may think of later on.

If you want a job or position for which you do not qualify, then qualify yourself by study. Take courses in the field you want to pursue or use the library facilities available to the public to teach yourself as much as possible about the job you want. Every worker or executive should constantly qualify himself or herself for a better position. Never stop upgrading your qualifications. Continually make yourself more qualified for better positions and better compensation. Study your job. Study the persons and the organization for whom you work. Learn from co-workers. Privates have become generals, and office boys have become company presidents in this way. As Adam Clayton Powell, Jr., said, "Learn, Baby, learn!" Never stop learning. Never stop qualifying and preparing yourself for greater things. Be ready and you will create your own opportunity.

To Review:

The first step in getting a job is to DECIDE you want to work. The next step is to DECIDE exactly what kind of job you want, then think about why you want the job. Make a list of all your positive qualities and how they will help you succeed at this job. Prepare for interviews by speaking the good you desire into existence. Prepare a neat, well-written résumé or summary of why you are qualified for the job and contact all the right people. Think in a positive and constructive way about yourself, and how you are going to benefit the company where you want to work. Improve your self-image. When you believe in yourself positively and correctly, then others will believe in you. And you will get the job or position you want.

QUOTES TO REMEMBER

"Everything that enlarges the sphere of human powers, that shows man he can do what he thought he could not do, is valuable."

~ Ben Jonson

"Learn, Baby, learn!"

~ Adam Clayton Powell, Jr.

"Never stop learning."

~ Rev. Ike

"When you look at the haves and the have-nots, you will see the dids and the did-nots

~ Anonymous

"Once you believe in yourself, you become unstoppable!"

~ Rev. Ike

AFFIRMATIVE TREATMENT

Say this positive affirmation every night before you go to sleep to bring the job you want into your experience!

Right here and right now I see myself in the job that I want.

The job that I am ready for is ready for me. I see myself in it!

I see myself giving of my time and effort gladly and lovingly.

I see myself qualifying for good things, wonderful things.

I see myself doing a good job, an outstanding job at everything I do!

Therefore, better positions come to ME and I keep moving from glory to glory in my work!

REVIEW QUESTIONS

1. What is wrong with having just a vague idea in your mind of the kind of work you want to do?

2. What do you do if you want a job for which you do not qualify?

3. Why is it important to appear neat and confident in a job interview?

4. What kind of person should your résumé portray?

5. How should you prepare for a job interview?

6. What is the value of constant learning?

Chapter 37

THE DIVINE ORDER IS IN ORDER

Dr. Frederick Eikerenkoetter

Acquaint now yourself with Him and be at peace, thereby good will come unto you. Job 22:21

A SCIENCE OF LIVING PRINCIPLE

The Divine Order is in order, and it's not going to get out of order.

Many times people look around in the world and they see so much disorder. They see war going on over here and hatred going on over there and suffering going on all over. And all of a sudden they shake their heads and say, "Why doesn't God stop this mess?" Well, let me give you a blunt answer to the question. To begin with, God didn't start this mess or any mess!

Some people have the idea that maybe there is a God in the sky who starts things and stops things. It's mankind who starts these wars and then prays for somebody else to stop them! There's no God in the sky who starts disorder and who stops disorder. If there is disorder, it means that for some reason or other, we got our minds out of Divine Order. And it's your individual business to bring your mind back to the attention of Divine Order.

Disorder Multiplies Disorder

Jesus said, "Come out of the world." This means bring your attention away from the world's business and bring your mind to center upon the truth of your being.

The Divine Order is in order. God's business is in order. God's affairs are in order. And if your affairs get out of order, then you are minding the world's business. You must pay attention to the Divine Reality. You must pay attention to the Divine Order. So stop looking around at the disorder in the world. Because the more attention you give to disorder, the more disorder you will bring into your life. If you want to keep order in your life, keep your mind in Divine Order.

THE DIVINE ORDER IS IN ORDER AND IT'S NOT GOING TO GET OUT OF ORDER. When you get your mind and heart in order, this causes everything in your experience to get in order and stay in order.

The Bible says, "As a man thinks, so is he." (Proverbs 23:7) Everything that happens in your own individual life is a result of the state of your mind. When you believe that there is a Divine Order, this brings order into your life.

The Effects of a Belief in Disorder

One time, a custodian at our church residence in the mountains of California put a sign on a light switch that lights the road coming up the mountain. And the sign said, "Out of Order." I passed it two or three times that day and I didn't say anything. The next morning when I got up I noticed that the plumbing had stopped working. I spoke to him about it, and I asked, "What's wrong with the plumbing?" He said, "Well, it's out of order." And then he said, "Oh my goodness, the vacuum cleaner is also out of order." Then a few other things got out of order. I said to him, "You'd better take that 'Out of Order' sign off of that light switch. That's what started it all." You see, his belief in disorder created more disorder! You have to watch your thinking because negative thinking can create disorder.

If some appliance stops working in your home, never put up a sign that says, "Out of Order," because your subconscious mind will accept that, and will produce more things that are out of order. I told the custodian, "If you must put up a sign on something to be adjusted, just put up one that reads 'To Be Adjusted.' But never, 'Out of Order.'"

Harmonize Your World

If you are experiencing disorder in your individual world — if you are experiencing hate, anger, tension, and anxiety, these are manifestations of your mental state, your belief about yourself. You must look within and discover God's Divine Order that is always in order. As you behold, contemplate, and become one with the God-in-you, Divine Order will express itself in your mind and in all of your affairs.

If you want to bring harmony and peace into your life, **it must begin with you.**

It is a fact of Mind Science that when you are right with yourself, everything in life will be right for you. As you experience harmony, love, peace, and joy through your knowledge of the Presence and Power of God within, this will cause you to vibrate harmony and love to everyone and everything in your life. Life will harmonize beautifully for you when you reflect the Divine Harmony, the Divine Order within you.

When you're at peace with yourself, everyone and everything will be at peace with you.

That is the wonderful thing about this philosophy. It teaches individuals to let God's peace, order, and harmony into their lives. When each individual expresses the love, peace, wisdom, and understanding that is the Divine Truth of each of us, there will be no more wars, no more disorder. Divine Harmony, Divine Order will reign throughout the world. The ONLY way to world peace is expressed in the words of the song: "LET THERE BE PEACE ON EARTH, AND LET IT BEGIN WITH **ME**."

QUOTES TO REMEMBER

"World peace begins with the individual being at peace with himself." ~ Rev. Ike

"Order is not pressure which is imposed on society from without, but an equilibrium which is set up from within." ~ José Ortega y Gasset

"The Divine Order is always in order." ~ Rev. Ike

"Thine eternal thought moves on, thine undisturbed affairs." ~ Hymn

AFFIRMATIVE TREATMENT

The Divine Order is always in order.

I AM in harmony with everyone and everything through the Presence and Power of God-in-me.

Peace, love, and harmony reign within my heart, my mind, and all my affairs.

I AM keeping my mind in the Divine Order.

Thank you, God-in-me.

REVIEW QUESTIONS

1. What do we mean by "Divine Order"?
2. If your life is in disorder, tense, and full of anxiety, what should you do?
3. Why is there disorder, war, and hate in the world? What should we do about it?
4. How can peace be brought into the world?
5. Why should you never put up an "Out of Order" sign?

Chapter 38

YOU CAN LEARN!

Dr. Frederick Eikerenkoetter

Take my yoke upon you, and learn of me... Matthew 11:29

A SCIENCE OF LIVING PRINCIPLE

Learn of the Divine Perfection that is within you — Health, Happiness, Love, Success, and Prosperity!

At one of my meetings, I was going down the aisles and a gentleman stopped me and began telling me about all his ailments. He said, "Oh, Rev. Ike, I've got rheumatism and I've got arthritis." He said, "You know, I'm at the age now where I'm due to have these diseases." And you know what I told him? I said to that man, "As a man thinks, so is he." (Proverbs 23:7) That man believed that once he reached a certain age, he **had** to get sick.

Do you know the reason some people get sick? Because they have learned to be sick. People get sick because they believe in sickness. They **learn** to be sick!

You know why you get old and feeble? Because you learn to get old and feeble. And whom did you learn it from? You learned it by watching other people over the years. And you know just how you're supposed to be bent over. You know you're supposed to have arthritis and rheumatism. And you know it's a stylish thing to talk about the problems you will have at a certain age!

Well, I want to tell you, the same way you have learned sickness, you can learn health. The Apostle John says to us, "Beloved, I wish above all things that thou mayest prosper and be in health…" (3 John 2) Because the Divine Truth of you is health. The Divine Truth of you is prosperity. The Divine Self within you is perfection!

Learn To Be Healthy!

Make no mistake about it, if you can learn to be sick, you can learn to be healthy. And you can learn to **stay** healthy. As a matter of fact, you **must** learn. You must learn health instead of sickness, if you want to be healthy.

Whatever negatives you have learned, you can unlearn!

Learn To Be Happy!

Some people learn to be sad and miserable. Some people even **expect** to be miserable! And because they expect it, that's exactly what they are!

In some churches, people even talk and sing about being miserable. They sing, "Sometimes I'm up, sometimes I'm down, sometimes I'm almost level with the ground." Even the devil doesn't get that low!

Learn to be happy! Learn to lift yourself up. Expect good to come to you, and that is what you will receive! That reminds me of a popular saying: "If there is half a glass of water, a pessimist will say it is half empty, but an optimist will say it is half full." Learn to be an optimist! Learn to be cheerful! Learn of the goodness that is already within you.

Learn Of Your Divine Self

When Jesus said, "Learn of me," He was not talking about the human self. He was talking about the Divine Self. Learn of the

Divine Self within you. Your Divine Self is happy and joyful. Your Divine Self is healthy, happy, loving, successful, and prosperous.

Learn Health, Happiness, Love, Success, and Prosperity. Learn that the Divine Self within you is perfection.

Learn To Help Yourself

Too many times, people want to change their conditions and their situations, but they don't want to learn how to do it for themselves. They don't want to learn to help themselves! They come to my meetings and they say, "Rev. Ike, I just came down here for you to heal me." Just like that old man said, "Well, Reverend, I know I'm at the age where I'm due to have these things, so I just came down here to have you heal me." He had learned how to be sick. He had learned how to get old and feeble. But he didn't want to learn how to be healthy! And he's got the nerve to come down here for me to heal him. His attitude is, "Don't tell me nothing about learning to be well. You heal me!"

I can help you best by teaching you how to help yourself. Remember, as long as a man has it in his mind that he's due to have negative things, he's going to have negative things. And not only that, he's going to have them more abundantly. He'll probably even get the rocking pneumonia and the boogie woogie flu!

In the Science of Living, we teach you to help yourself. We teach you that through the consciousness of the Presence of God — Infinite Good — already within you, you can help yourself to live a positive, healthy, happy, successful, and prosperous life. Through the Divine Presence within you, you can unlearn sickness and know health. You can unlearn poverty and misery and know prosperity and joy. Because the God-Power within you is perfection. And as you become aware of this Divine Perfection, as you learn to help yourself, you will leave poverty, failure, and sickness behind!

QUOTES TO REMEMBER

"Just as people learn to be sick, miserable,   ~ Rev. Ike
and poor, they can learn to be healthy,
happy, and prosperous."

"The tongue of the wise is health."   ~ Proverbs 12:18

"Unlearn sickness, and know health!"   ~ Rev. Ike

AFFIRMATIVE TREATMENT

I open my mind to the Presence of God-in-me, the Divine Perfection
   within me.

I unlearn sickness and I learn Health!

I unlearn sadness and I learn Happiness!

I unlearn hatred and I learn Love!

I unlearn failure and I learn Success!

I unlearn poverty and I learn Prosperity!

I AM one with the Divine Perfection within me.

Thank you, God-in-me!

REVIEW QUESTIONS

1. How do people learn to be sick? How can you learn to be well?

2. What is meant by the word "unlearn"?

3. What will happen when you learn to expect good in your life?
   Why?

4. Do you look at life with an optimistic or pessimistic attitude?
   (Refer back to the popular saying about the glass of water.)

Chapter 39

THE INFINITE ECONOMY

Dr. Frederick Eikerenkoetter

As a man thinks, so is he. Proverbs 23:7

A SCIENCE OF LIVING PRINCIPLE

You must learn to deal with the economy that does not economize. You must learn to deal with the infinite economy of God within.

We've been hearing a lot about the economy over the past couple of years. Experts have been suggesting many different things, trying to figure out what would be the best thing to do to improve the economy. People have come up with some amazing ideas, and I want to analyze some of them now and put them to rest.

Economic Fallacies

Some people have the idea that perhaps it will cure the material economy if each of us uses less. They suggest that by using less we will have more. But that is a fallacy. A fallacy is just a dignified way of saying "lie." It is a fallacy to think that by using less we will have more.

There are two fallacious statements that I would like to debunk. It is a fallacy to think:

- That by enjoying less we will have more.
- That by giving up or not having good, that this self-denial will help other people.

You must learn to deal with the economy that does not economize. You must learn to deal with the infinite economy of God within.

Let's Turn the False Beliefs Around

Now let's turn all of the fallacious beliefs around, and make them positive beliefs.

Correct use and correct enjoyment appropriate more to use and to enjoy.

You see, I'm talking about the psychological economy of the subconscious mind. This is why I teach you to use and to enjoy the good which you do have. The more you use and the more you enjoy the good which you have, the more good you will create for you to use and to enjoy. That's why I'm constantly telling you, "Don't save your good dishes until the preacher comes to visit." Take your good things out and use them — enjoy yourself! Don't ever think that anything is too good for you! If all you have left in your pocket right now is a dollar, do something with that dollar that you will enjoy. Bless it and enjoy it.

The enjoyment of good increases and multiplies the good.

Whether you have a little or whether you have much, enjoy. My Jewish friends and associates use that word "enjoy" as a parting greeting that always turns me on. They'll say to me, "Enjoy!" And it does something good to me. And it should do something good to you. That greeting should release the joy potential within you. Remember, the Infinite within you takes many forms, and one of the many forms it takes is joy. You have within you unlimited joy potential. And you should let it express itself.

You Are Always Dealing With the Infinite Economy

You see, people forget that they should enjoy life. They talk instead about austerity. They talk about using less. They talk about enjoying less. But those of us who understand mind science know that we are always dealing with the Infinite. We know that through the Infinite Presence and Power of God within, we can always appropriate an abundance of good. If you could grasp this Truth, your problems of supply in any form would be over.

I'm always dealing with the Infinite. I'm not dealing with anything that there's not more of.

Everything that there's a so-called shortage of right now, there is more of it. Even the so-called oil shortage turned out to be a lie. And when all of you were cutting back and complaining that you couldn't get enough gas, I refused to participate. While the whole world was having its gas shortage, I had the whole freeway to myself. Because you see, I'm dealing with the economy that will not economize. I'm dealing with the kind of economy that Jesus knew. Didn't Jesus say, *"My kingdom is not of this world"?* (John 18:36) It's the same thing that I'm dealing with — unlimited economy. "My economy is not of this world."

When you learn about this infinite economy, shortage won't come near you. The other folks will have their cars parked on the sides of the road and you and I will share the freeway.

Don't Cut Back

Another fallacy the experts tell us is that we should start doing without the extras of life. This is what they mean by "austerity." They tell us we should start practicing "cut-back living." But if we start doing without, if we start buying less, then everything cuts back, and the economy gets worse!

When I tell you to live abundantly, that doesn't mean to live wastefully. Living with the extras does not contradict efficiency. I define efficiency as making the most of everything — including time, effort, materials, manpower, and mind power. And to live an abundant life, you have to be efficient in the use of your mind. Choose what you're going to be, do, and have, and what you're not going to be, do, and have. And do not use your mind on any idea that does not promote health, happiness, love, success, and prosperity.

You have to decide what you want to be, to do, and to have, and look to the Infinite Source within, and you will find the infinite economy.

QUOTES TO REMEMBER

"Back of the loaf is the snowy flour,   ~ Malthie D
And back of the flour the mill,   Babcock
And back of the mill is the wheat and the shower
And the sun and the Father's will."

"Correct use and correct enjoyment appropriate   ~ Rev. Ike
more to use and enjoy."

AFFIRMATIVE TREATMENT

I believe in the infinite economy of the Presence and Power of God-in-me.

I deal with the economy that will not economize, with a belief in the abundance of all things.

I get what I want in abundance.

I AM established in opulence and luxury, through the Presence and Power of God-in-me.

Thank you, Father!

REVIEW QUESTIONS

1. Will giving up luxuries improve the economic conditions of the world?

2. What is "the psychological economy of the subconscious mind"?

3. How does the enjoyment of good multiply good?

4. Is there an oil shortage? Why or why not?

5. Discuss the following words: austerity, appropriate, efficiency.

Chapter 40

HOW TO STOP CATCHING DISEASE

Dr. Frederick Eikerenkoetter

The tongue of the wise IS health. Proverbs 12:18

A SCIENCE OF LIVING PRINCIPLE

Health or sickness; wealth or poverty; success or failure — all begin in the mind. Your physical body and material affairs reflect your state of mind. The person with a positive attitude and a strong belief in health prevents sickness from entering his life.

Most people have been mentally conditioned to accept sickness from the beginning of their lives. From the minute you are born, you are taught to believe in sickness. You learn that you are supposed to be sick at certain times of the year. You learn that you are supposed to be sick at various times of your life. You learn to believe in the very idea of sickness.

While you are growing up, your parents expect you to get a whole catalog of diseases that the so-called medical authorities say children are supposed to catch. You are supposed to have the measles and the mumps, the whooping cough and the chicken pox. Your parents expect you to get these diseases, and you expect to catch these diseases. And if you don't catch these diseases in succession, one right after the other, something is WRONG with you!

Most parents have unconsciously conditioned their children to expect sickness. I remember when I was a child, whenever I sneezed, my mother would tell me that I was catching a cold. And without fail, every time I sneezed I would end up catching that cold. In fact, I was so conditioned by this childhood experience, that for years, every time I sneezed, I would subconsciously hear my mother saying, "You're getting a cold." That simple statement had an effect on me until I learned to master my own thinking.

I learned that if I stopped thinking sickness and stopped expecting sickness, that I would stop getting sick. And I learned to block any idea of sickness out of my mind and out of my life.

Sickness Is For Never

People are taught that they will come down with one illness or another at certain times of the year. At the beginning of winter every year, for example, the national disease center in Atlanta decides what disease everybody is going to have that year. They announce it on television so that you'll know what to catch. And every year they give the disease a new name. One year it's the Hong Kong flu. The next year it's the London flu. The next year it's the grippe. The next year it's the Asiatic flu. Every year they tell us what epidemic we're going to have. And whenever you look in the newspaper, you read about how this disease is spreading. Every time you turn on the radio or television, the announcers give you the statistics on how many people have it. Some little old ladies catch it from the newspapers. Some people catch it from the radio. And some people catch it from the eleven o'clock news!

People catch the disease the national disease center plans for them, because they <u>expect</u> to get it. They <u>believe</u> in their minds that they will get it. They read all about the symptoms — they get all wrapped up in how miserable this disease will make them feel — they put all of their attention into how long this disease will last — until it's no wonder that they get it!

Right Thinking and Speaking

Most people are just too interested in what's wrong with them and what's wrong with the world. They give negative ideas all of their attention, and negative conditions continue to enter their lives. I am always warning you that the more you give your attention to negative conditions, the more negative conditions you will have. The more you think and talk about your symptoms and your aches and pains, the more symptoms and aches and pains you are going to have.

It is very important to only let your mind think positive thoughts about health. It is very important to only let your mouth say positive things about health. Watch what you think or say, lest you become "ensnared by the words of your mouth." (Proverbs 6:2) Never think thoughts such as, "I think I'm getting a cold," or "I'll never get over this sickness." These negative thoughts cause you to get sick and prevent you from getting well. Instead, say to yourself on a regular basis, "I AM healthy and I will stay healthy... **God-in-me is my health.**" This positive affirmation heals you and keeps you well.

So if you don't want the disease that the national disease center plans for you this year, refuse to believe in it. Refuse to take part in any idea of sickness. Say to yourself, "God-in-me is my health." Learn the mastery of your own mind and your own thinking, and the negative beliefs entertained by the world-mind will no longer influence you.

Unlearn Sickness and Know Health

Since we've all been taught to believe in sickness, now we have to work at unlearning sickness. We have to learn how to be healthy and stay healthy. In the Science of Living, we teach that each individual has the potential to be healthy and happy, to love and be loved, to be successful and prosperous. But many people prevent themselves from attaining good health, happiness, or success by the negative ideas they have about themselves in their minds. Once you come to know the Truth of you, you will know that the way to a healthy, whole mind, body, and soul is through identification of yourself with your True Self, the Presence and Power of God within you.

God individualized Himself within you and within each man. Your True Self is your God-Self, the Presence and Power of God-in-you.

The way to achieve health is to identify yourself with the Presence and Power of God within you. You and your Father are one. Identify yourself [become aware of your "oneness"] with all of the good that God is.

The Presence of God-in-you is healthy and whole. *"I wish above all things that thou mayest prosper and be in health."* (3 John 2) It is God's highest desire that you be a healthy, whole individual. It is God's highest desire that you become aware of your ONENESS with Him — of your oneness with health, happiness, love, success, and prosperity.

One of my favorite healing testimonies in this Ministry is an example of what positive identification with the Presence of God within can do.

A young man attended one of my Healing and Blessing Meetings at my Church in New York City. He was sitting in the congregation before the meeting began. And as I walked down the aisles as I usually do to meet and greet the people, this youngster leaned over from his seat and said to me, "Rev. Ike, please pray for me. I have asthma." I stopped for a moment and looked at him and said, "Son, I see in you a boy who has no asthma."

Not long after, this young man told me a wonderful story. He said, "Rev. Ike, that Sunday when you said to me, 'Son, I see in you a boy who has no asthma,' something lifted from my chest, and I've never suffered from asthma since."

What happened? I caused him to identify with his healthy self — with the healthy, whole Presence of God within him. When I said, "I see in you a boy who has no asthma," he got a picture in his mind of himself as being healthy, as having no asthma. He identified himself with the Presence and Power of God within. He became aware of his oneness with God, and he was healed.

You can become healed and healthy by accepting the healthy, whole Presence of God-in-you. You can change your experience from one of sickness to one of health, by believing in the image of yourself as a healthy, whole individual — by identifying yourself with the Divine Image of health.

This is one of the interesting things about this Ministry — we not only heal people but we also teach them how to stay healthy. We not only help people out of disease, but we teach people how to maintain their health. So you see, you don't have to be sick in order to benefit from what I'm teaching. When you learn to identify yourself with health, when you stop accepting sickness, this prevents sickness from even entering your life.

THINGS TO THINK ON

It is important to make healthy thinking a habit. The positive affirmation, "God-in-me is my health," should be used over and over until it becomes part of your thinking. Start each day by saying to yourself, "God-in-me is my health." During the day, whenever the world-mind tries to feed you the idea of sickness, reject it by remembering the healthy, whole Presence of God-in-you, and saying to yourself, "God-in-me IS my health." Repeat this to yourself before going to sleep at night. The more you repeat this, the more you will impress the idea of health upon your subconscious mind.

QUOTES TO REMEMBER

"Your True Self is your God-Self, the Presence of God within you."   ~ Rev. Ike

'The tongue of the wise IS health."   ~ Proverbs 12:18

"God-in-me is my health."   ~ Rev. Ike

AFFIRMATIVE TREATMENT

Right here and right now, I see myself as a healthy person.

I refuse to accept any idea of sickness.

My faith and belief are in God's healthy, whole idea of me, and this belief will keep me well.

God-in-me is my health.

God-in-me heals me and keeps me well.

Thank you, God-in-me for health!

REVIEW QUESTIONS

1. How was the young boy with asthma healed?

2. Can you prevent yourself from getting sick? How?

3. Can people actually catch a disease from reading the newspaper? Why or why not?

4. Why are some people troubled with sickness during their lives?

Prayer of Inoculation for Health

Right here, right now,
I make up my own mind,
I decide for myself, that I don't want,
That I don't need,
Any of these old sicknesses and diseases.

In God's mind I am healthy.
I am an expression of God Itself.
And I don't want anything that is not like God.
I don't have to have any of these diseases that the
World says I'm supposed to have.
And I throw that idea of sickness and disease out of my mind.
Out, out, out, out, OUT!!

I say to sickness and disease:
"Hit the road, Jack, and don't come back no more!"
I say to any sickness and disease
That the world says is on the way:
"I've got my blockade up for you —
Detour!!
I don't want you, I don't need you.
You're not welcome, you're no good."

Now that I have cast out all of these false ideas,
I open myself to the truth of God.
I accept God as my healing,
Right now, right now, right now.
I accept God as my continual good health!

God is my health:
Health in every bone,
Health in every muscle,
Health in every organ,
Health in every limb,
Health in every function,
Health in every tissue,
Health in every atom,
Health in every part of my being.

Therefore, there is no room for anything else to get in.
I am inoculated by the Presence of God-in-me.
I am inoculated from sickness and disease
By the Presence of God-in-me.
And so it is, from everlasting to everlasting,
God is God-in-me, through me, and as me.
And I rejoice because of it!

Chapter 41

HOW ARE YOU MEETING LIFE?

Dr. Frederick Eikerenkoetter

Keep thy heart with all diligence: for out of it are the issues of life.
Proverbs 4:23

A SCIENCE OF LIVING PRINCIPLE

Your attitude is the most important thing about you. Your attitude determines your experience.

Many people don't realize that their attitude toward life is very important. But your attitude is very important! It can make you or break you! Your attitude determines your experience in life. Your attitude determines how people respond to you. Your attitude determines if you will be a success or failure in life.

How Your Attitude Affects Your Life

Now when I talk about attitude, I mean your mental approach to life. Your attitude is your disposition toward yourself, other people, and things.

First, let's observe how your attitude affects your life. When you wake up in the morning, do you drag out of bed and moan, "Oh my God, another day. I sure hate to have to go to work. I sure hate to meet that mean old boss of mine." Or are you one of those people who say, "Oh, I sure feel bad today. Sure wish I didn't have to get up. Sure wish I didn't have to go out of the house today."

If these are your first thoughts in the morning, your attitude toward life is negative. And when you finally do get up and go out to meet the world, your whole day probably turns out bad! You go to work and your bad attitude makes you grumpy. And that makes your boss even meaner, and the next thing you know, he fires you!

There's no telling what you will meet in life if you go out in a negative mood and with a negative attitude. The people around you will sense it and withdraw from you. Nobody wants to be around somebody who is sour all the time. I don't want to be around anybody who is sour any of the time!

Life Meets You Like You Meet Life

Now let's see what happens if you turn that negative attitude around. How do you think your day would be if, when you wake up in the morning, you shouted, "THIS IS THE DAY WHICH THE LORD HAS MADE, I WILL REJOICE AND BE GLAD IN IT!!!" That would shock your emotions into the right attitude, wouldn't it?

It might be too much for some of you to shout at yourself first thing in the morning, so some of you calmer types can try this: Every morning when you wake up, start thinking about the plans you have for the day. Say to yourself, "I have opened my eyes and I am going to get up now. I am going to go out into the world and I will perhaps meet hundreds of people. I am going to meet them positively and joyfully. I am going to meet many kinds of conditions, circumstances, and situations, and I am going to meet each of them equally positive and joyful. I am going to have a good day. Thank you, Father!" You try this. It will work for you, I know it.

Life is going to meet you today and every day just like you meet life.

In this philosophy we are not dealing with blind faith or dumb luck. This philosophy is a science. It is a technology for living, because it teaches you how to determine the results that you are going to achieve in life; it teaches you how to determine the circumstances and situations in your life. Every day, you can meet life knowing if your day is going to be successful or not by first asking yourself, "How am I going to meet life today?" How you answer that question will determine your day.

Do You Have A Positive Attitude, Every Day?

Getting up in the morning and facing life with the right attitude is only one part of learning how to meet life properly. The other part is learning how to maintain that right attitude throughout each day — throughout every situation and condition you face. Now I'm not just talking about keeping a smile on your face. Attitude goes a lot deeper than that. It is a state of mind.

Notice your attitude throughout the day. Are you a positive person? Are you getting caught up in your problems or your neighbors' problems, or are you finding answers? Are you cheerful and pleasant to be around?

When you meet life cheerfully, life will meet you that way. Your positive attitude will cause everyone and everything to respond to you in a positive way.

Let me give you an example. How many of you have ever had a dog? Maybe you've been away at the office all day and you drag home dead tired, and there he is — just waiting to greet you! He barks and jumps up to tell you how happy he is. He's so excited to see you that you can't help but respond to him.

And that is the way life is. If you meet life with enthusiasm and with the right attitude, life has to respond to you the same way. The Cosmic Law of Mind states, *"As a man thinks, so is he."* (Proverbs 23:7) It cannot be otherwise.

Improve Yourself

If you want to improve your experience of life, you must do something positive with your attitude, you must work at how you think. And you have to stop thinking that someone else will come along and change life for the better for you. In the final analysis, "No one can do your doing but you." No one can change your life for the better but **you**.

This may be a little bitter for some of you to swallow. But in this philosophy there are no scapegoats. There is no devil to blame. In this philosophy, "You are your own devil, you are your own God. Only you can choose the path you trod."

I can give you these techniques, but you have to use them and work with them. You have to decide to help yourself to have a better experience in life. So when you wake up in the morning, always ask yourself this question, "How am I going to meet life today?" And remind yourself that life is going to meet you just like you meet life. Use this technique to start your day right. Decide to meet life positively, with a smile on your face and joy in your heart, and you will find that joy and happiness become part of your experience.

Get in the habit of programming yourself every morning for health, happiness, love, success, prosperity, and money. Practice talking yourself up! Say, "This is the day which the Lord has made, I will rejoice and be glad in it." Think positive thoughts, and develop a positive attitude toward life. It will take five minutes, ten minutes, or maybe fifteen minutes a day, but it's worth it If you go into life with a healthy, happy, loving, successful, prosperous idea in your mind, life will meet you with all these good things.

QUOTES TO REMEMBER

"Life is going to meet you just like you meet life."   ~ Rev. Ike

"The secret of life is never to have an emotion that is unbecoming."   ~ Oscar Wilde

"No one can do your doing but you. No one can change your life for the better but you."   ~ Rev. Ike

AFFIRMATIVE TREATMENT

Right here and right now, life meets me exactly as I meet life.

Therefore, I meet life with an enthusiastic attitude.

I meet life with a joyful attitude.

Joy and enthusiasm send out positive vibrations to everyone and everything in my experience, and my joy and enthusiasm are reflected back to me.

I program myself every day for health, happiness, love, success, prosperity, and money.

Thank you, God-in-me.

REVIEW QUESTIONS

1. What is attitude?

2. What are some techniques for determining the kind of experiences you will have each day?

3. What does your attitude have to do with your experience in life?

4. What kind of attitude do you wake up with each day? How can you improve it?

5. How does life meet YOU? What are you doing about it?

Chapter 42

YOU HAVE MULTIMILLION-DOLLAR TALENTS!

Dr. Frederick Eikerenkoetter

I am the Lord thy God, who teaches you to profit, who leads you by the way that you should go. Isaiah 48:17

A SCIENCE OF LIVING PRINCIPLE

The Infinite Mind of God which is within you provides you with an infinite variety of ideas and talents. It is up to you to open your mind and accept these ideas. And it is up to you to receive them.

Many people think that in order to improve themselves financially, they have to start with some grandiose scheme, with plenty of financial backing. But I want you to think for a moment about the beginnings of the financially successful people you have read about and the tycoons of industry and business. Most industries and businesses start with just an idea and an individual who had enough faith in that idea to develop it. Some of you have talents and ideas that could also be the foundation of multimillion-dollar operations.

One of the basic premises of this Ministry is that the Presence and Power of God are within each of us. When you accept the Presence of God within, you realize that the Mind of God — with Its infinite ideas and creative power — is also within you.

Open your mind to the Presence and Power of God-in-you, and you will discover money-making ideas. **Open your mind to accept the God-in-you**, and you will be surprised what wonderful things you will discover. You will find money-making ideas, right ideas, coming to you from all directions. Even if these ideas seem simple and mundane to the conscious mind, they have the potential to make you rich.

Some time ago, a man had the idea to sell peanuts and cold drinks at baseball games. And if you've been to a baseball game recently, you know how these types of businesses are prospering. Some of the great restaurant chains and some of the large hotel chains also had small beginnings. For instance, the Marriott Corporation, a multibillion-dollar corporation, started as a summer root-beer stand at a baseball stadium. And look at it now!

Henry Ford built his first gas engine out of scrap material that cost about a dollar!

You Have an Area of Expertise

God has given every person some talent, some area of expertise. There is no person whom God has forgotten. But it is up to the individual to accept God within and let his area of expertise be revealed to him.

One of my favorite money-making success stories is of Colonel Sanders. He learned to fry chicken. That was his area of expertise. That was his forte. I just love the story of Colonel Sanders' success. He dropped out of school when he was in the sixth grade. He was wiped out of one business when he was sixty-five years old. And then with only a one-hundred-and-five-dollar social security check, he took his talent at frying chicken and built a multimillion-dollar food franchise.

I know some people who can out-fry Colonel Sanders' chicken every time. And I want to ask them, "Why aren't you rich?" Many people can fry chicken, but they find some excuse to blame for their failure. Maybe they say, "Well, I don't have an education." Now what that has to do with being successful at frying chicken, I don't know. You see, people think of all the reasons why they can't succeed and prosper instead of opening their minds to success and recognizing the money-making ideas and talents already within them. They say, "I don't have enough money to start a business," or "I don't know how to develop this idea." They talk themselves out of their good ideas. They talk themselves out of their success and their prosperity!

Too many people complain so much about the opportunities they don't have that they don't see the ones they do have!

Take another multimillion-dollar idea, the big McDonald's hamburger chain. While other big corporations are going bankrupt and folding up, Kentucky Fried Chicken, McDonald's, and other popular fast-food chains are booming. The McDonald's founders had one simple idea: the fast hamburger. Colonel Sanders had a simple idea: fried chicken. Some of you make better hamburgers and better fried chicken, and I want to ask you again: "Why aren't you rich?"

Amos's Cookies

There is a young black man in Los Angeles who is making a fortune baking cookies. He makes all kinds of cookies. He used to bake cookies for his friends and take them with him wherever he went. When he visited his friends, he would take them his cookies to sample. And his cookies were so good that his friends had him making more and more cookies. Then the idea hit him, "Hey, I'll put this on the market!"

His cookies are so good, that his business is flourishing. He has been written up in the New York Times and a lot of other publications. Success stories like this really turn me on, so recently I made a special trip over to his cookie shop. He told me how big stores like Bloomingdale's in New York, for example, are placing orders for his cookies. He ships his cookies all over the world. And anybody who tastes one of his cookies is hooked on them.

You, too, have multimillion-dollar talents. You, too, have multimillion-dollar ideas.

Right Ideas Through The Presence Of God Within

I wrote this lesson and gave you these examples because I want to make you aware of some of the simple things that have made millions and billions of dollars for other people. Simple ideas have made people rich. A simple idea can make you rich!

Many times we scorn the simple talents and the simple abilities that we have. We discount ourselves. This is why I keep reminding you of the Presence and Power of God within. The Presence of God within you is your source of right ideas. Through the Presence and Power of God-in-you, you have money-making ideas and talents that can make you rich. The Mind of God-in-you is always giving you new ideas, wonderful ideas, right ideas that can make you successful. Open your mind to the Divine Mind within. Accept the ideas which the Infinite has to offer. Have faith in yourself, and you can't lose.

Once you have an idea, don't ask "how" it will come about. It would be a cruel and unkind God to give you the ability to form ideas, and at the same time withhold from you the ways and means to bring your ideas into manifestation. When you believe in and trust God-in-you, you will discover the ways and means, the *modus operandi* to achieve what your mind has conceived. Thanks to God-in-you, the idea and the means are already within you. It's up to you to accept these right ideas and to use them positively and correctly.

THINGS TO THINK ON

Keep a notebook with you at all times, and every time an idea comes to you, jot it down. Frequently review these ideas to see how you can turn them into money-making ideas for you.

Make a list in this notebook of the types of things you do best. Do you have any hidden talents? Don't be modest! Analyze your abilities. What talents do you have that you can develop into a money-making operation?

QUOTES TO REMEMBER

"There is a thing stronger than all the armies in the world: And that is an idea whose time has come." ~ Victor Hugo

"You have multimillion-dollar talents; you have multimillion-dollar ideas." ~ Rev. Ike

"If a man has a talent and cannot use it, he has failed. If he has a talent and uses only half of it, he has partly failed. If he has a talent and learns somehow to use the whole of it, he has gloriously succeeded" ~ Thomas Wolfe

"Those who dare, do; those who dare not, do not." ~ Anonymous

AFFIRMATIVE TREATMENT

Right here and right now, I acknowledge that the God Presence within me is my infinite source of good ideas.

God-in-me gives me the ideas and the talent to make me successful in all that I endeavor.

Everything that I do prospers.

God-in-me acts through me, in me, and as me to bring my good ideas into creation.

I have multimillion-dollar talents.

I have multimillion-dollar ideas.

Thank you, Father.

Thank you, God-in-me!

REVIEW QUESTIONS

1. With what did many prosperous industries and businesses start?

2. Do you need lots of money to start a money-making operation? Why or why not? What is a "grandiose scheme"?

3. Where do your multimillion-dollar ideas come from?

4. How will your ideas be brought into creation?

5. What is your multimillion-dollar idea or talent?

Chapter 43

ACHIEVING YOUR IDEAL FIGURE

Dr. Frederick Eikerenkoetter

And the Lord answered me, and said, Write the vision, and make it plain. Habakkuk 2:2

A SCIENCE OF LIVING PRINCIPLE

You can use the power of your mind to bless and direct your physical body and affairs.

You don't have to be overweight or out of shape to benefit from this lesson. The techniques in this lesson will help you to lose weight, to keep weight off, to maintain physical fitness, and to keep a slim and trim figure regardless of age. But you must continue to practice these techniques for them to continue to work for you.

Over the years I have developed these techniques for maintaining my physique. I use them myself, and now I want to give some of them to you. When I decide I need to slim down, I go to the magazine stands regularly and buy every physique magazine I can find. I go through them carefully and open them to the pictures of people who look the way I want to appear. I lay some of these pictures around me on the floor, and I put some up on the wall all over the house. No matter which room I go into, I'm always looking at the type of physique that I want to have. What happens is that my subconscious mind is continually impressed with the idea of a slim and trim me. And consequently I trim down.

This technique will work for you, too. Get all the fashion magazines and health magazines you can find. Find pictures of the ideal figure that you would like to have, and place those pictures where you can see them every day. Put them on the floor and on the walls of all the rooms you frequent during the day. If you cannot spread magazines and photographs throughout your house, place them in your own private section of your room or house.

Select Your Ideal Figure

Ladies, select pictures of the type of feminine figure you would like to have. Maybe you would want to get Seventeen magazine, so that not only are you selecting a petite figure, but you're selecting a youthful appearance as well. And when you focus your attention continually on the figure you want, remember what I tell you, "What you see is what you get!" Not only that, but "What you see is what you become." Your subconscious mind will record what you impress upon it and will bring it about. Your subconscious mind records everything, and brings it into manifestation. If you keep pictures of youthful beauties before your eyes, you will become like them!

Men, do the same. Select your ideal physique from men's fashion magazines and health books. Now I personally don't want to be a "muscle man." So, I select certain ideal photographs of figures that represent to me only my ideal profile. I don't surround myself with pictures of "muscle men," because I don't happen to want to have the physique of a muscle man. And you have to be careful of this, because your subconscious records EXACTLY what you impress it with and will bring that to you accordingly.

So select your ideal. As the Bible says, "Write the vision, and make it plain." You have to make it plain to your subconscious mind exactly what you want to be, to do, and to have.

Be Specific

If you want to lose or gain weight, it is important to **be specific** about how much weight you want to lose or gain.

I'll tell you what happened with me. While I was growing up, I was skinny. I wanted to gain weight, but no matter how much I ate, I never gained weight. I never could gain weight until I was about twenty-two. And then I got my subconscious mind turned around to gaining weight, but for awhile I didn't think to turn it off. You see, that's what you have to be careful about. Because your mental process is, in a sense, just like an automobile. It's not enough to get the car going; you have to know how to regulate it, how to control it. You have to know how to stop it when it should be stopped. And many times in our lives we get things going and don't know how to stop them. It took me the first twenty-two years of my life to start gaining weight. Then I got my mental processes going in the direction of gaining weight, but didn't install any stops or controls. I kept gaining weight because all I said to my subconscious mind was, "I want to gain weight." I couldn't stop gaining because I wasn't specific about how much I wanted to gain!

Never simply say, "I want to lose weight," or "I want to gain weight," and leave it there. Never do that! Why? Because you are starting an action but providing no controls. When you get in your car, you wouldn't dare get in your car without knowing how to control it. You're going to use the brakes, the steering wheel, the accelerator — you're going to keep that car under your control. You're going to drive it in specific directions under your control. So, once again, never simply say, "I want to gain weight; I want to lose weight." Because you have left the situation open. You haven't been specific. **There must be a clear picture in your mind.** You should select exactly how many pounds you want to weigh, and have a picture in your mind of the ideal figure you want to have.

You Can Tell Your Body How to React

All of this that I am teaching you is part of the principle that I taught in my sermon-lesson, "Tell Your Body How to React." Once you learn how to use your mind power, you can shape your body at will. You can take off the pounds you want to take off, and put on the pounds you want to put on. Once you learn to use your mind to control your body and all of your experiences, you have become a master. That's the meaning of the word "master." You're master of your own fate, and captain of your own soul, when you know how to use your mind to control your experience in life.

QUOTES TO REMEMBER

"What you see is what you become!"   ~ Rev. Ike

"Our life is what our thoughts make it."   ~ Dale Carnegie

AFFIRMATIVE TREATMENT

Right here and right now, I have found the Power within me to control all of my experiences.

I see myself strong and healthy from birthday to birthday.

I AM becoming the ideal figure I want to be.

I AM the master of my fate and the captain of my soul.

So it is, it cannot be otherwise, and I rejoice because of it.

Thank you, God-in-me!!!

REVIEW QUESTIONS

1. How can the principles in this lesson be applied to life in general?

2. What happens when you surround yourself with pictures of the physical build you desire to have?

3. Why should you never just say, "I want to gain weight," or "I want to lose weight"? What should you say?

4. Can you shape your body at will?

5. When have you become a "master"?

6. What is your ideal weight? Can you see yourself with the ideal weight you want to achieve?

Chapter 44

STOP THE WORLD, I WANT TO GET OFF!

Dr. Frederick Eikerenkoetter

Greater is He who is in you than he that is in the world. 1 John 4:4

A SCIENCE OF LIVING PRINCIPLE

Through the Presence and Power of God-in-you, you can leave negative living behind, and experience the joys and riches of life.

Have you ever been to a carnival and watched the horses on a carousel go round and round? Each horse is traveling in the same direction, but they all are traveling in a circle, getting nowhere. Sometimes this is the way life seems. We keep covering the same ground, but we never make any progress. So in this lesson, I want to discuss the merry-go-round of life and how to gain control of the reins. To put it in the words of a popular song, we say, "Stop The World, I Want To Get Off! I'm Tired Of Going Round And Round!"

First, let me define the word "world." In the Science of Living, "world" refers to the "world-mind" — all of the negative ideas, negative thoughts, and negative attitudes of mankind. The Science of Living teaches that if you get caught up in the negativism of the world, you will experience negatives on the individual level. So the words "Stop The World, I Want To Get Off! I'm Tired Of Going Round And Round" suggest that if you are tired of experiencing negatives, you should get off the merry-go-round of negative world beliefs. You should get out of the habit of believing everything the world-mind has to say — get out of the habit of accepting what the world-mind says. You should stop your mind from accepting negative information from the outside world. This is getting off the merry-go-round of negative world beliefs.

Negative Ideas in The World-Mind

What are some of the negative ideas the world-mind believes in? The world-mind believes in lack and limitation. The world-mind believes in poverty. And if you are tired of going round and round in poverty, in lack, and in limitation, you've got to get off this negative merry-go-round. You've got to decide, "I'm going to stop this mess. I'm going to get off this negative merry-go-round of lack, limitation, and poverty."

I got off the merry-go-round of poverty. I said, "Stop this mess, I want to get off!" I said, "I'm tired of going around in this poverty circle. I'm tired of going around in this lack and limitation circle. I'm tired of going around in this culturally deprived circle." And so I stopped that negative merry-go-round and got off.

In the Father's business, you can never be unemployed.

The world-mind believes that there is an unemployment problem. And that's another negative concept that just goes around and around in the world-mind. But in the Science of Living we learn that if you would just be about the Father's business, you would never be unemployed. The Father's business is always booming. The Father's business is knowing yourself correctly, knowing who and what you are in God and who and what God is in you. The Father's business is being positively self-motivated. A person who believes in himself correctly and who is correctly self-motivated will never be out of a job.

Get Off the Negative Merry-Go-Round of Sickness

If you aren't careful, the world will really confuse you. It will tell you when to be sick, it will tell you what kind of disease to have, it will tell you when and how to die. This belief in sickness is another part of the merry-go-round of negative thought. If you want to be well and stay well, you have to get off this negative merry-go-round.

Every year the world-mind has some seasonal disease for you to get. There is a national disease center in Atlanta, Georgia, and they study the kind of diseases that are coming each season. Every year in the fall we are officially told what kind of disease we're supposed to get that winter. A few years ago it was the Hong Kong flu. Then it was the Asiatic flu. Then it was the grippe. Every year they predict a flu epidemic, and every year people get the flu in epidemic proportions. Some people catch a disease from just listening to the suggestion of it on the radio. Some people catch a sickness from reading about it in the newspapers. And some little old ladies catch a disease from the eleven o'clock news.

If you want to maintain health, you have to get off the negative world-mind merry-go-round. The next time the national disease center tells you what disease you're going to have, you must say, "I will have nothing to do with that." When the news announcer on television begins to talk about how many people have gotten the flu, you must tell the world-mind, "I have nothing to do with that." Anything that you don't want, shrug your shoulders and wave your hand and affirm, "I have nothing to do with that."

"Be ye not conformed to this world."

Don't let the world-mind tell you how to think or how to feel. Don't let anybody tell you why you can't be, do, and have all the good you desire.

Beware Of Ungodly Counsel

The Bible tells us, *"Walk not in the counsel of the ungodly."* (Psalms 1:1) Now that means the same thing that I'm telling you. "Ungodly counsel" is the negative world belief in poverty, sickness, and failure. "Ungodly counsel" is anything that tells you why you **can't** be, do, and have the good you want. The newspapers are at least 90 percent "ungodly counsel." The eleven o'clock news is at least 90 percent ungodly. Any belief in negatives is "ungodly counsel." "Walk not in the counsel of the ungodly" means to call your mind out of the negative beliefs of the world-mind. Listen to the Divine Counsel, the voice of God, the voice of Good, within you.

Call Your Mind Out Of the World

If you want to experience a life of health, happiness, love, success, and prosperity, you have to learn how to get out and stay out of the world's negative business. As an individual you must call your own mind out of the negative beliefs of the world-mind. You must focus your attention, your belief upon the Divine Presence, the Divine Power within you. When you pray, when you meditate, your attention should be on the Presence and Power of God-in-you. Call your mind out of the world and focus upon the Divine Presence within you.

Any kind of negative merry-go-round you're on, know that through the Presence and Power of God-in-you you can stop it and get off.

The Bible says, "My house shall be called a house of prayer." (Matthew 21:13) What house does this refer to? It is the house of your mind. The house of your mind should be a house of positive prayer where positive thoughts gather. Keep your mind out of the world's negative business, and into the positive business of God — the business of Infinite Health, Happiness, Love, Success, and Prosperity.

QUOTES TO REMEMBER

"Stop The World, I Want To Get Off!"   ~ Popular Song

"A person who believes in himself correctly   ~ Rev. Ike
and who is correctly self-motivated will
never be in negative circumstances."

"Be not conformed to this world, but be   ~ Romans 12:2
transformed by the renewing of your mind."

AFFIRMATIVE TREATMENT

Right here and right now, I stop the negative world-mind merry-go-round.

I get off the merry-go-round of negative thought.

I have nothing to do with the world's bad luck.

I have nothing to do with lack and limitation.

I have nothing to do with poverty.

I got off of all those negative merry-go-rounds and I'm not getting back on.

I AM going to stay off through the Presence and Power of God-in-me.

I AM being what I want to be, doing what I want to do, and having what I want to have.

I AM out of the world's business and into the Father's business, of Health, Happiness, Love, Success, Prosperity, and Money!

Thank you, God-in-me!

REVIEW QUESTIONS

1. What is the difference between the business of the world-mind and the Father's business?

2. What is the *"ungodly counsel"?* What is "the world-mind"?

3. How do the national media perpetuate the negative world belief in sickness?

4. What kind of thoughts should you gather in the house of your mind?

5. From now on, what are you going to do when you are confronted by the world-mind belief in poverty, sickness, lack, or limitation?

Chapter 45

A TECHNIQUE THAT DOES THE TRICK

Dr. Frederick Eikerenkoetter

When men are cast down, then thou shalt say, There is lifting up.
Job 22:28

A SCIENCE OF LIVING PRINCIPLE

The goals that you achieve in life are a direct result of the way you feel about yourself.

There is a very rich and successful man who fascinates me with the way he begins every day. Every morning he says, "I feel good, I feel great, I feel terrific!" And I'm sure that if some of you heard a grown man, a business executive, a multimillionaire, going around shouting, "I feel **good**, I feel **great**, I feel **terrific!**" you'd probably say, "Well, he's just getting old and senile." But for years this man has used this technique to "lift" up his feelings. And he has taught his sales staff and his organizational people to use this technique also. It inspires them to go out and SELL! And today he has a multimillion-dollar insurance company that is **very** successful!

He begins staff meetings by having everyone say, "I feel terrific!" Then they sing an old Sunday school song that goes, "I feel the joy, joy, joy, joy down in my heart." These are the techniques they use to get excited about their business and their lives. And it is so important to be excited about your life and what you are doing.

In this lesson I'm going to give you some techniques that will lift you up, techniques that will help you get excited about life, techniques that will bring into your life the good desires of your heart. But first I want to define the word "technique." **A technique is a method for accomplishing a desired aim — a method for accomplishing a practical purpose.** So in this lesson, I'm going to give you methods for achieving and maintaining health, happiness, love, success, prosperity, and money.

Lift Up Your Feelings

Some people don't know why they are unhappy or why they feel so bad. They go around with their feelings dragging in the dirt. They go to a psychiatrist for ten years and pay him umpteen thousand dollars and he still can't tell them why they feel bad. But you see, happiness doesn't just happen. You've got to learn to feel happy. You have to tell your feelings how to feel. You should always affirm, "I feel **good**! I feel **great**! I feel **terrific!**"

A lot of people ask me, "Rev. Ike, how can I say I feel good if I don't feel good?" When your feelings are dragging, that is the very time you ought to say, "I feel good, I feel great, I feel terrific!" Your positive words will impress your subconscious mind and prepare the way for you to feel happy and to feel good. **You see, telling your feelings to feel good is the technique that does the trick.**

Feeling right about yourself uplifts your whole experience in life.

When you lift up your feelings, when you feel happy, you will find happiness in everyone, everywhere. Life is like a mirror — it reflects back to you a perfect image of yourself. Create in your mind a feeling of joy, a feeling of happiness, and an expectation of good, and you will discover joy, happiness, and good everywhere.

Techniques For Every Day

I remember one morning, for some reason I woke up in a blue mood. There was a phonograph right beside the bed with a good shouting gospel record on it. So I turned on the phonograph. And when that music began to play, I made one leap out of bed and started singing and dancing. I got out of that blue mood. I got out of that blue mood by lifting up my feelings.

Find yourself a good song to sing in the morning. Find a good "shower song" — a song to sing while you're in the shower. And this will have a two-fold effect on you. You'll be cleansed both inside and outside.

Whatever you do to lift your feelings will lift up your experience and your enjoyment of life. If listening to a particular piece of music makes you feel better, that is a good spiritual and mental technique to practice. Everyone should develop his own mental techniques. You should practice positive mental techniques. If it does not hurt you, does not harm anyone else, and helps you to lift your feelings and your experiences, it is a good spiritual and mental technique.

Here is another technique: When you wake up in the morning ask yourself this question, "How do I feel about myself?" When I talk about "feeling," I mean discover your basic "gut" feeling about yourself. Cross-examine yourself and ask yourself, "What is my 'gut' feeling about myself?" Ask this of yourself regularly, because the most important thing in life is to establish how you feel about yourself. You must establish a feeling of health, a feeling of happiness, and love, a feeling of success and prosperity at the "gut level" of your feelings. That's the technique that will do the trick!

Establish a feeling of health, happiness, love, success, and prosperity in your mind.

Be sure to program your feelings before you go to sleep every night. Go to sleep feeling right about yourself, about everyone, and everything. Make peace with yourself in your own mind. And you will prepare yourself for positive experiences when you wake up the next day.

I don't want you to think that what I'm teaching you is something you can do without any effort. This is sort of a do-it-yourself religion, a do-it-yourself philosophy. You have a lot of work to do — I give you good positive techniques to practice — but you've got to practice them every day. You've got to work to change. You can't lose with the stuff I use! And as you work to change your feelings, you will change your whole experience in life. As you use the techniques I am giving you for establishing a positive feeling about yourself, your positive experiences in life will increase.

THINGS TO THINK ON

Use this technique tonight and every night before you go to sleep. Ask yourself the question, "How do I feel about myself?" And then say this affirmation to yourself:

I feel good, I feel great, I feel terrific! I feel the healing Power of God-in-me flowing in my body, mind, and soul. I feel happy about myself. I feel loved. I feel loving. I feel successful. I feel prosperous. I AM full of the money feeling.

Whatever you want in life, get full of the feeling of already having it As Rev. Ike says, "Fulfeelment will bring fulfillment." Your subconscious mind will work out its own ways and means and lead you into being, doing, and having the good which you desire.

QUOTES TO REMEMBER

"If you tell me how you get your feeling of importance, I'll tell you what you are. That determines your character. That is the most significant thing about you."   ~ Dale Carnegie

"If you feel right about yourself, you can do anything!"   ~ Rev. Ike

AFFIRMATIVE TREATMENT

Right here and right now, I lift up my feelings about myself.

I tell myself, "I feel wonderful!"

My positive feeling about myself is uplifting my whole experience in life.

I feel right about myself, about everyone and everything.

I let go of any negative feeling about myself and anyone else.

The Presence of God-in-me is my Infinite Source of All Good.

And I feel wonderful!

REVIEW QUESTIONS

1. Personal question: "What is the 'gut feeling' I have about myself"?

2. What is the definition of the word "technique"?

3. What are some techniques other than those discussed in this lesson for lifting up your feelings?

4. When is one of the most important times to lift up your feelings? Why?

A SAVIOR

I am one that believes in you
    It makes no difference what you say or do
For within your soul I see a plan —
    The pattern of a heaven man.
I'm a savior when I see
Perfection coming forth in thee
When others knock and pull you down
I upon you never frown,
    But hold to "that" above your par
The heaven man you really are;
    For when I see you truly great
I wipe illusion off your slate
    And help you to see with me
The vision clear that sets you free.
    For you are "That" — The Perfect One —
GOD'S Beloved Only Son;
    So stand erect and believe in you
For you really are, The Master, too.

Retsama

Chapter 46

ARE YOU READY FOR WHAT YOU WANT?

Dr. Frederick Eikerenkoetter

Behold, I send my messenger before your face, who shall prepare thy way before you. Matthew 11:10

A SCIENCE OF LIVING PRINCIPLE

Whatever you are ready for, is ready for you.

Some people say, "Rev. Ike, I want this…" or "Rev. Ike, I want that…" and they can't understand why they never get it. They don't understand that if you are not mentally ready to receive something, you will never receive it.

If you want to experience the good you desire, it is not enough to just hope for it, or wish for it. You must get ready to receive it. You must prepare yourself to receive it. **Because whatever you are ready for is ready for you.**

Are You Ready?

Every time you think of the good that you want, ask yourself, "Am I ready to receive the good I want?" Because when you are ready for it, it will happen. When you get yourself ready for the good you want, when you mentally prepare for that good desire, the Presence and Power of God-in-you will bring it about.

I have developed certain techniques for mentally preparing myself for the good that I want. And if you use these techniques, you will find that the good you are ready for is ready for you.

Don't Ask How

You may not understand how these techniques work, but it really doesn't matter if you understand all the mechanics behind them or not. They will work whether you understand the mechanics or not. For example, I don't understand everything about how a car works, but when I get into one of the Church's Rolls Royces and turn the key, it starts right up, and I go where I want to go. That Rolls Royce doesn't know that I don't understand all the mechanics and it doesn't care. It will work whether I understand the mechanics or not. And so it is with the Law of Mind. It works whether you understand all the mechanics behind it or not.

Whatever you mentally prepare yourself for, the Cosmic Law of Mind proceeds to produce it. And the Law of Mind will produce it with ease. If you don't have the money for the new car you want or the new clothes you would like, don't go beating your head against the wall worrying, "How is this technique going to work? How will I ever get the money I need?" Use these Science of Living techniques to prepare yourself for the good you desire. Mentally prepare yourself for the new car, or the new clothes, or whatever the good is that you want. And then relax. You will be inspired and motivated to do what you need to do to get what you want.

1. Techniques For Receiving A New Car

If you want a new car, stand in front of your house, or in your driveway, or wherever you are going to park it. As you stand in the place where you want your new car, visualize yourself sitting comfortably in the driver's seat. Feel yourself driving in your car. Put your hands on the steering wheel and imagine yourself turning corners. Feel the notches behind the steering wheel. Get "full of the feeling" of driving your new car.

As you sit in your car, smell that new car smell. Smell that luxurious leather interior. Now push the buttons that roll the windows up and down, and listen to some soft music on the radio. Relax in the driver's seat and accept the new car in your experience.

You see, by visualizing yourself with your new car in this way, and by getting "full of the feeling" of having and driving your new car, you are preparing yourself to receive that car. You are preparing yourself to have that car in your experience.

2. Techniques For Expanding Your Wardrobe

If you want new clothes, prepare yourself to receive them. Go and clean your closets to prepare a place for them. Even if you can't see the ways or means right now to buy a new wardrobe, organize your closet. Get yourself ready to receive. Get some wardrobe organizers. Get holders for the shoes that you own, but leave space for the new shoes. If you don't have enough money to buy wardrobe organizers, put some clean newspaper on your shelves and line the bottom of your dresser drawers. Prepare yourself to receive and increase your wardrobe.

What does all this do? Organizing yourself for a new wardrobe prepares you to receive it. You're making room for the good you desire — you're preparing yourself for the good you want!

Your actions mentally prepare you to receive new clothes and new shoes. And whenever you prepare yourself mentally for some-thing, the Cosmic Law of Mind will proceed to produce it!

These techniques will work with whatever good you desire. Apply these techniques to your needs and your wants. If it is a house, a higher education, a new job, a promotion in your present job, a vacation, or more money that you need, prepare yourself to receive it. Make room in your experience for the good you want to come to you.

3. Always Be Ready For Right Ideas

Here is a third technique to prepare yourself to receive. This may seem like a very simple and a very mundane technique, but I cannot over-emphasize its importance. **Always carry with you something to write with and something to write on.** This way, when a good, prosperous idea comes to you, you are ready to write it down and ACT upon it. And I'll guarantee you that the mental and physical action of being ready for right ideas will precondition you to receive. Being prepared will make positive money-making ideas come to you from all directions.

Be Careful Of Negative Preparation

When you are preconditioned to receive only good, not even trouble will come to you. Trouble will not come into your life unless you have prepared for it in some way. This reminds me of a young man who had an illness and went to the hospital. When he got out, he said, "You know, I sure learned a lesson that time. I didn't save up any money. When I get back to work, I'm going to save up some money so that the next time I get sick and go to the hospital, I'll have some money to pay for it."

He got well and went back to work. And he worked real hard and saved his money, so that the next time he had to go to the hospital, he would have some money. And sure enough, he got sick again, and had to go back into the hospital. He said, "Oh, it sure is good I saved up this money to help me pay my doctor and hospital bills."

And he got well from that illness and went back to work and worked hard again, to save some more money so that when he got sick and went back to the hospital, he'd have enough money. And he went back to the hospital a third time. Then he realized what he was doing to himself and stopped.

What was he preparing himself for? He was preparing himself to get sick and go to the hospital! He was conditioning himself for sickness — he was ready to get sick! If you prepare your mind for negatives, sure enough, just like that old doleful hymn says, "that

248

awful day shall surely come, that appointed hour makes haste." Whatever you mentally prepare yourself for "shall surely come" to you. So be sure to prepare yourself only for good. Prepare yourself and be ready to receive the good you desire.

QUOTES TO REMEMBER

"Whenever you mentally prepare for   ~ Rev. Ike
something, the Cosmic Law of Mind
proceeds to produce it."

"Mind is the great lever of all things."   ~ Daniel Webster

AFFIRMATIVE TREATMENT

Right here and right now I prepare myself for good.

I AM ready to receive the blessings and riches of life.

The good I am ready for is ready for me.

Thank you, Father.

Thank you, God-in-me!

REVIEW QUESTIONS

1. How can you prepare yourself for the good you desire? List some specific techniques.

2. What good are you preparing yourself to receive? How?

3. Why did the man in the story get sick and go back to the hospital three times?

4. When is the good you desire ready for you?

5. Will the Law of Mind work for you if you do not understand the mechanics behind it?

Chapter 47

YOU REAP WHAT YOU SOW

For Thanksgiving

Dr. Frederick Eikerenkoetter

For with the same measure that you measure, it shall be measured to you again. Luke 6:38

A SCIENCE OF LIVING PRINCIPLE

You must learn how to give, before you can receive. Just as in nature when earth gives forth its bounty it gives seed for the next season, we must learn to plant the seeds for our harvest of health, happiness, love, success, and prosperity.

Fall is the time of year when, in the cycle of nature, the earth gives forth her harvest. It is the time when we reap that which we have sown. And Thanksgiving is a special day when we thank God for so richly multiplying our blessings. But, we should give thanks every day for all the abundance God has brought into our lives.

The Lord shall open unto thee His good treasure.

That you must sow [give] in order to reap [receive] is a universal law of nature, a law of life. This law holds true in all relationships. Just as the farmer must give seed to the earth to receive a harvest, you must give to life in order to receive life's blessings. You must learn how to give first, before you can get God's blessings of health, happiness, love, success, and prosperity. If you desire God's abundance, you must learn to give abundantly. I always say that the secret of living is giving, because giving demonstrates your faith. When you give generously to good causes that you believe in, you show your faith!

There Is No Such Thing As Something For Nothing

People are always looking for a "free lunch," or a "free ride." But as economist John Kenneth Galbraith has said, "There is no such thing as a free lunch." There is no such thing as receiving something for nothing!

Nothing is free — not even the air you breathe. You cannot take another breath until you give away the one you have!

Give, and it shall be given unto you.

The Lesson of Right Giving

This is a very hard lesson for some people to learn, but those who learn to give right find that giving opens their lives to receiving the blessings of God in abundance. Whenever you give correctly, your giving does not take from you, but rather it causes you to be blessed. Take, for example, the wild flowers of the field. They crop up all over the countryside in springtime. Every year they give all their bounty back to the earth, and they are multiplied until the fields are covered with their beauty, more and more every year.

When the farmer plants seeds, he gives seeds to the ground, and he gives his time and effort to till the soil. He works to make his seeds multiply so that he will harvest an abundance of fruits and vegetables from the seeds he plants. The farmer receives a multiple of what he has given. He plants a single seed of corn, and he receives an entire stalk which in turn will produce more corn. This multiplying law of nature is what is meant by the saying, "Anyone can count the seeds in an apple, but only God can count the apples in a seed."

God is generous, and He gives back to you a multiple of what you give. People in this Ministry who plant "Money Seeds" by giving regularly to good causes, receive wonderful blessings. As they continue to give, their blessings increase and are multiplied. They find out that God within is a generous God.

God loves a cheerful giver.

A certain businessman and his wife heard me talking on right thinking and right giving and they sent me a donation. Before they had learned the lesson of right giving, they had been having trouble getting the money that was due them. But after they planted their "Money Seeds" and showed their faith by giving to a good cause, they were blessed with almost A QUARTER OF A MILLION DOLLARS. Now, they continue to give from that they receive, and this opens their lives to more receiving.

He who soweth sparingly shall reap also sparingly; and he who soweth bountifully shall reap also bountifully.

You Must Prime The Pump

There is an old folk tale about a man who is lost in the desert and dying of thirst. By chance he finds a rusty water pump. He tries to pump the old thing, but nothing happens. No water comes out to quench his thirst. Then he notices beside the pump a small jug of water with a note from an old prospector. The note reads, "You have to prime the pump with water, Friend." Now, the man was really thirsty and needed water badly. He considered just drinking the water out of the jug, but then he decided to trust in the old prospector's advice, instead. He poured the whole jug of water down the rusty old pump. He began to pump it again, and this time the water gushed out! But he had to give before he could get. "Whatever you need, give some of it away," someone has said. If you want more love, give more love. If you want more happiness, contribute to the happiness of others (after you become happy with yourself).

This means you must give from what you receive to keep receiving. It is the same with the farmer. When the farmer receives a harvest, he cannot use his entire harvest — he must set aside the seed from his crop to give back to the earth so he can reap another harvest. The farmer must give good seed to receive a good harvest.

There cannot be any kind of receiving until there is some kind of giving. Employees must first give their service before receiving pay. Somebody must work before those on public welfare can receive their assistance. So even those on "welfare" do not receive "something for nothing." Their dole comes out of the working peoples' paycheck.

Is Your Source Limited?

Some people ask, "How long can I keep receiving my blessings?" This is the secret: God-in-you is your unlimited source of All Good. When you believe in God-in-you, when you have faith in your unlimited source and give freely and generously, you set up a flow of giving and receiving that will never stop! It will only stop if you stop giving and believing.

God-in-you is a God of **abundance**, an unlimited source of good. Jesus said, "I have come that you might have life and that more abundantly." Those who learn the lesson of right giving are discovering the secret to abundant living, and are experiencing the abundant flow of blessings in their lives.

QUOTES TO REMEMBER

"Nothing is free, not even the air you breathe. Before you receive another breath, you must give up the one you have."

~ Rev. Ike

"For it is in giving that we receive."

~ St. Francis of Assisi

"Life takes from the taker and gives to the giver."   ~ Rev. Ike

"God loves a cheerful giver."   ~ 2 Corinthians 9:7

"Whatever you need, give some away."   ~ Anonymous

AFFIRMATIVE TREATMENT

I AM giving in good faith to causes I believe in. My giving does not take from me — through giving I prosper even more.

Blessings of health, happiness, love, success, and prosperity are pouring into my life through the Power and the Presence of God-in-me.

Thank you, Father!

Thank you, God-in-me!

REVIEW QUESTIONS

1. Explain the universal law, "You reap what you sow."

2. What is "right giving"?

3. How does the law of giving and receiving work in matters of love and happiness?

4. What are "Money Seeds"? How do they work?

5. What does the expression mean: "There is no such thing as a free lunch"?

6. How many blessings can one person have?

HOW SWEET IT IS

How sweet it is,
This life divine;
Guided and protected,
Lifted to heights unknown.
Reaping a harvest of good
Long since sown.

How sweet it is,
The way the Spirit unfolds
In life,
Sparing all who listen
From ill begotten moments
Of sorrow and strife.

How sweet it is!

By Elizabeth Vear

Chapter 48

FORGIVE YOURSELF

Dr. Frederick Eikerenkoetter

But this one thing I do, forgetting those things which are behind, and reaching forth unto those things which are before, I press toward the mark.... Philippians 3:14, 15

A SCIENCE OF LIVING PRINCIPLE

Forgiveness starts with you. You must forgive yourself and get rid of your negative feelings of self-condemnation. Live in the knowledge of the truth of you — your Divine Self that never sins — and leave all guilt behind.

Some people, deep down in their hearts and minds, hold a grudge against someone or something. People hold things against themselves. I know of people who pray and pray for years, asking God to forgive them for things they were involved in or did years before. They hold their past mistakes against themselves and it affects the rest of their lives.

Some of you made one mistake long ago and continue to feel guilty about it! Maybe you have loved ones who have passed on, and although you did everything you could to help them, in your hearts and minds, you're still worrying, "I wonder if I did everything I could?" These feelings add up to what is called a guilt complex.

In this lesson I'm going to teach you how to get rid of your guilt complex. If you are feeling guilty about something within your heart and within your mind, you are asking for punishment and you are going to get it!

You Must Forgive Yourself

As long as you hold negative things of the past against yourself, you will hold yourself down into a rut, down into a negative pattern where you will continue to repeat your mistakes. The Bible says, "He that covers his sins shall not prosper, but whoso confesses and forsakes his sins shall have mercy." (Proverbs 28:13) This means that if you're going down the wrong road and you know you're going down the wrong road, it's not enough for you to say, "I'm going down the wrong road" and continue to do so. You must acknowledge your mistakes. You must forgive yourself for your mistakes. You must forgive yourself and change your ways. You must turn around and go the right way!

When a person deep down in his own heart and mind fails to forgive himself, he thinks that God does not forgive him. If you feel that God has not forgiven you for your mistakes, it is a sure sign that you have not forgiven yourself.

I want to repeat this again because this is what some of you need in order to set yourself free from a guilt complex: if you feel that God has not forgiven you for your past error or your past misdeeds, it is a sure sign that you have not forgiven yourself. **The Almighty will not hold anything against you that you repent of, if you forgive yourself.**

Jesus said, *"Neither do I condemn thee; go, and sin no more."*

A Guilt Complex

Psychiatrists call man's failure to forgive himself a "guilt complex." The guilt complex is one of the main causes of mental disease. I know of people in Beverly Hills and Hollywood who spend years and years and thousands and thousands of dollars on psychiatrists' couches trying to get rid of a guilt complex. During my last seminar in

California I taught them about forgiveness and saved them millions of dollars! And it helped the psychiatrists there also, because the psychiatrists have more patients than they can handle.

You see, sometimes people get rich so quickly they can't adjust to their new-found prosperity. They become stars so fast that they can't adjust to their new-found success. Maybe they've been taught to be ashamed of having money, and so they feel guilty for the money they have. All this adds up to the same thing — a guilt complex.

A guilt complex always brings punishment. A guilt complex compels and draws punishment.

Search Your Mind

If negative things keep happening to you, you had better search your mind and see if you have a guilt complex. If you discover you do have a guilt complex, then settle it in your own mind and settle it quickly. Because as long as you have that guilt in your mind, it's going to draw punishment to you. And it will draw punishment to you from sources and from people that seem completely unconnected to you.

Guilt in the mind can draw punishment in so many different ways that you won't have the slightest idea what the cause is. This brings to mind a song that I use from time to time to demonstrate this. It's an old so-called spiritual that says, "I wonder what I have done to make my race so hard to run." It could be that you're going around with a guilt complex. Be sure that you settle the guilt question in your own mind. Be sure you settle any negative thoughts in your own mind so that you can begin enjoying positive experiences in your life.

Stop Persecuting Yourself

Some people have the habit of persecuting themselves, and saying, "Oh, why did I do this!? Oh, why did I do that!?" If you are persecuting yourself for something that you did or something that happened long ago, stop it. Never indulge in self-persecution. Because self-persecution brings on self-depreciation, self-rejection, and spiritual disease.

If you have been apologizing to God and praying, "Lord, forgive me, forgive me Lord, please forgive me," stop it! THERE IS NOTHING YOU CAN DO ABOUT YOUR PAST MISTAKES BUT FORGIVE YOURSELF. Forgive yourself for your past mistakes and forget them! Stop judging and condemning yourself for the sins you believe you have committed. After all, who hasn't done things he regrets? Who hasn't made mistakes? God forgives you **when** you forgive yourself, and turn from your error.

In order to be what you want to be, do what you want to do, and have what you want to have, you must look to the God-in-you for the strength you need to forgive and forget your past mistakes and recognize the truth of you — your Divine Self that never sins. This truth of you — your Divine Self — will give you the strength to stop dwelling on the negative things, will set you free from any guilt complex you might have, and will start bringing the good desires of your heart into your life right here and right now!

QUOTES TO REMEMBER

"You had better learn how to forgive yourself and how to forget past mistakes. This isn't yesterday, this is today."

~ Rev. Ike

"Better by far that you should forget and smile than that you should remember and be sad."

~ Christina G. Rossetti

"When you forgive yourself, and turn from your error, then God forgives you."

~ Rev. Ike

AFFIRMATIVE TREATMENT

Right here and right now, I forgive and forget all of those I think have wronged me in the past.

I let go of any grudges deep down in my heart and I forgive myself for the mistakes I have made.

I forgive myself and I forget my guilt!

I cancel guilt from my mind and I look to the God-in-me for health, happiness, love, success, and prosperity.

Thank you, God-in-me!

REVIEW QUESTIONS

1. What is a guilt complex, and what does it draw to you?

2. Why must you forgive yourself?

3. Discuss these terms: self-condemnation, self-persecution, self-depreciation, self-rejection.

4. Can God forgive us if we don't first forgive ourselves?

Chapter 49

HOW TO PROGRAM YOUR LIFE

Dr. Frederick Eikerenkoetter

Be you transformed by the renewing of your mind. Romans 12:2

A SCIENCE OF LIVING PRINCIPLE

If you don't program your own life and mind, the world-mind will.

We are all familiar with the recent "scare" in the country when it was announced that so many thousands of people were going to die next year from the swine flu. Now who had ever even heard of "swine flu" before then? And all of a sudden a big program was started to inoculate people on a mass basis against the swine flu. The world-mind created this negative idea and gave it to you.

The world-mind tries to program you with negatives. Last year, two of the negative ideas you were programmed with were strain "B" flu and a bad economy. Now I'm going to tell you something that will shock you. A lot of people probably got colds last year and **thought** it was the flu. They had heard so much about how the flu was spreading and they read all about the symptoms. So they went to bed **prepared** to get really sick with the flu, and they did! They were programmed with all the negative symptoms, and they got them! There were also people who were **afraid** to apply for jobs last year because they *thought* there weren't any jobs available — so they didn't even try to find one. This is the extent to which people let the world-mind program their lives with negative ideas.

You have to learn to program your own mind and your own experiences in a positive way. That is why I say, the hell with the swine flu! I refuse to accept the idea of it! I refuse to be programmed for it! Let the world-mind have it, because I don't want it.

What Is Programming Your Life?

Did you ever stop and think about who or what is programming your life? Every one of us is programmed, including me. But the important thing is to have control over how you are being programmed. Ask yourself, "Who or what is punching MY buttons?" Are you programmed by the world-mind, or do you program yourself? Are you programmed by what OTHER people believe, or do you do what you believe to be right?

The world, other people, and conditions will play with your mind if you let them. To live the kind of life you want, to enjoy health, happiness, love, success, and prosperity, you have to program your own thoughts and your own experiences. If you are letting other people's ideas program you and your life, you have to stop doing that. Get rid of those old, negative ideas! Do not permit your mind to be programmed by T.V., newspapers, or any part of the mass media.

Do You Let Circumstances Program You?

If you find yourself saying, "I would like to do such and such a thing, I'd like to be such and such, I'd like to have such and such… BUT under these circumstances, I can't…," you're permitting circumstances and conditions to program your thinking, to program your ideas of what you can or cannot be, do, and have. You are not programming yourself. You have to decide for yourself what you want to be, to do, and to have.

When you decide what you want, never consult the circumstances. Never let anything stop you from getting exactly what you want. Some people will say, "As soon as I get some money, then I will decide what I want." Decide what you really want now, and that decision will compel all the ways and means of getting what you want.

Even if you don't have a nickel, plan what you will do with the money you receive. If you are sick and you want to reprogram your life out of sickness into health, decide that you want to be well.

"Let every man be fully persuaded by his own mind."

Program Yourself for Good Things

Your experience of prosperity begins with your decision to prosper. Don't ever talk yourself out of prosperity. If I had done that I'd still be walking barefoot on the muddy roads of South Carolina. And the people in those big, long cars would still be splashing mud on me. No, I decided then, as a young boy, that I was going to have one of those big, long cars myself. I programmed myself for prosperity instead of identifying myself as a poor little black boy in the mud.

Say "I AM"

While I was in poverty, I programmed my life for prosperity. This is the way it works.

The Bible tells us, "Let the weak say I AM strong." That's programming your life, that's programming your mind positively. It follows that the poor should say, "I AM successful! I AM rich!" The sick should say, "I AM well!" This is one technique for programming your life. Whatever you add to "I AM" you become.

When you say "I AM" it is like programming a computer. You are the computer — a storehouse of unlimited potential. The "I AM" selects and prepares you to become whatever follows it, whatever you add to it. Now the most expensive, up-to-date computer is no good unless you know how to use it properly. Unless you program it properly to get exactly the information you want, you're wasting your time and effort. When you add a negative to "I AM," you are wasting your potential. If you say, "I AM a poor minority," you're not using your computer in a positive manner.

When you blindly accept what the world-mind has programmed for you, you are wasting your potential. You're using the world-mind's computer instead of your own. But when you say, "I AM talented! I AM going to be successful!" you are making good use of your computer. You are programming and preparing yourself for a successful, prosperous life. And, when you say, "I AM healthy," "I AM rich," you are programming and preparing yourself for health and riches.

Flatly Reject What You Don't Want

Another technique for programming your life as YOU want it is to flatly reject what you don't want. Know that you don't have to have what you don't want. If failure is suggested to you, reject the idea. At the beginning of this lesson I gave an example of this. I said I didn't want any part of the swine flu, I simply rejected it. Flatly rejecting what you don't want is powerful. If you ever catch yourself giving attention to a negative trend of thought, stop and get yourself out of it. You have to reaffirm that you can be, do, and have the good you want. Grab a hold of yourself, and shake yourself into believing that the good you want will come into your experience.

Too many people let other people program their lives for them. You have to learn how to encourage yourself, and how to program yourself. When you discover how to program your own mind and your own life, then wonderful things will open up for you!

QUOTES TO REMEMBER

"You always get compensated for your attitude."   ~ Rev. Ike

"Man is not the creature of circumstances. Circumstances are the creatures of men."   ~ Benjamin Disraeli

AFFIRMATIVE TREATMENT

Right here and right now I program my life for good.

I refuse to be programmed by circumstances and conditions. I reject any negative ideas from the world-mind.

I program my mind only for good.

I accept Health, Happiness, Love, Success, and Prosperity in my mind and in my life.

Thank you, Father.

Thank you, God-in-me!

REVIEW QUESTIONS

1. What happens if a person does not consciously program his own mind?

2. How is the recent "swine flu scare" an example of world-mind programming?

3. How do radio, T.V., newspapers, and other parts of the mass media program people's minds?

4. Give two techniques you can use to reprogram your life.

5. When is the time to program your life for prosperity? For health? For all good?

6. How much and how often should a person work on programming his mind for the good he desires?

Chapter 50

YOU CAN GET THERE FROM HERE!

Dr. Frederick Eikerenkoetter

You shall know the truth, and the truth shall make you free.
John 8:32

A SCIENCE OF LIVING PRINCIPLE

The only thing you need to know is yourself. When you know yourself, then you'll know everybody and everything you need to know. All your good desires will be fulfilled.

We all know that some people seem to struggle and strain through life more than others. Some people think that God loves one person more than another. Some people think that some other person is holier than they are. But let me tell you. LIFE DOES NOT GIVE MORE GOOD TO ONE PERSON THAN IT CAN GIVE TO ANOTHER.

If life seems to be unfair to you, it is because you have not opened yourself up to receive! ALL good is already present. ALL GOOD IS READY FOR YOU TO ENJOY! WHEN YOU OPEN YOURSELF UP TO RECEIVE, YOU WILL HAVE AND ENJOY ALL THE GOOD THINGS IN LIFE.

How to Get the Good You Desire

You should want and enjoy all the good things in life — the things that make life more enjoyable. This power to have the good you desire is within you. It is within easy reach if you understand the universal principles that are involved — the principles of mind science.

Once you accept the principles of mind science, you can use them to be, to do, and to have what you want. In fact, it is not even necessary to understand how they work. Years ago Thomas Edison was asked what electricity was. He said, "I do not know, but I use it." And man has used electricity ever since to make life easier and more enjoyable. The principles of mind science are the same — they are there for you to use. Mind science will work for you as you accept it, believe it, and work with it.

The Bible says, *"He [the Lord, the Law of Mind] is no respecter of persons."* (Acts 10:34) That means that the Law of Mind will work for you — not just for the rich, not just for the poor; it will work for everybody who works with it.

What Are The Principles Of Mind Science?

The basic principles of Mind Science are set forth in the following Bible verses.

"As a man thinks so is he." (Proverbs 23:7) This means that as a man thinks of himself, so he experiences life. If a person thinks sickness, failure, poverty, unhappiness, and hate, he brings these things into his life. If a person thinks positively about himself, mentally identifying himself with Health, Happiness, Love, Success, Prosperity, and Money, he draws these things into his life!

"Be you transformed by the renewing of your mind" (Romans 12:2) is the Mind Science Key for changing one's experience. It means that if you want a new experience — get a new idea of yourself; change your life by changing your self-image. You only need to change *your mind about yourself*, and "things" will change

267

— not till then. You don't need to change "the world" or "others." Change *your* mind, change *yourself* and others will change. Or at least you will be so different that it won't make any difference.

Jesus stated the basic law of Mind Science thus, *"According to your faith, so be it unto you."* (Matthew 9:29) Your faith is what you believe about yourself. Therefore believe the truth about yourself. Believe your Divinity. Accept your Divine Sonship, *"And all these [good] things shall be added unto you."* (Matthew 6:33) The truth of man (every man) is that he is the Son of God.

The purpose of Mind Science is to teach one to know and think positively about himself, and thus, bring good to himself and others.

Mind Science teaches man to build and maintain an image of himself in his mind *already* being, doing and having the good he desires. This ideal self-image in the mind inspires and motivates the one in whose mind it dwells, and commands the good which it mentally represents. The self-image leads to its own fulfillment.

"You shall know the truth, and the truth shall make you free." (John 8:32)

You shall know the truth of who you are in God and who God is in you. This truth that we deal with is not a religious truth as such. It is not a dogmatic, doctrinal truth, it is the truth of *you*. It is the truth of each individual — the truth of all mankind. Once you accept the Presence and Power of God-in-you, you can travel the path of self-discovery. You can be entirely in control of your life. You can be the person you want to be, you can do what you want to do, and you can have what you want to have.

"Know Thyself"

Too many times, people go all the way through this experience of life and come to know so many different facts, but they never come to know their true identity. Stop and think about it! How much do you know of your true identity, and how do you apply that knowledge to your everyday life? Rev. Ike usually says, "You don't know anything until you know yourself. When you know yourself, you'll know everybody you need to know and everything you need to know. All that you desire will come about." Let me emphasize that:

The only thing that you really need to know is yourself. When you know yourself, then you'll know everybody you need to know and everything you need to know. All you desire will come about.

Centuries ago, William Shakespeare wrote it another way: "To thine own self be true. And it shall follow, as the night the day, Thou canst not then be false to any man." (*Hamlet* I, iii, 75)

The puzzle of life and the truth of man have occupied man's thoughts for centuries. Over the door of the Temple of Apollo at Delphi in ancient Greece, these immortal words were inscribed: "Know Thyself." That is a big challenge, but self-discovery IS possible, and it can be done.

It Is Your Responsibility

It is your responsibility to discover your true identity. This is your responsibility as an individual. Today especially, so many people are searching for what they call their "true identity." Many times they give themselves an identity by accepting a label or "stamp" that someone else has put on them. It is rather popular, for example, for people who are monetarily poor to identify themselves by saying, "Well, I'm underprivileged." But I'm telling you that if that is the identity you give yourself, you're in trouble.

You must decide for yourself who you are and what you want out of life. You must not unquestioningly accept the label or stamp that the government agencies and other groups give to you.

Not only do you have within yourself the God power of self-discovery, you have the responsibility for self-discovery. No matter where you are in your life, stop and ask yourself these questions:

269

What do I want to be?
What do I want to do?
What do I want to have?

And don't compromise on the good you want. Answer each question with the very highest thoughts and desires you have. Because once you've answered these questions, you will continue up the path of self-discovery. You will begin the process to be, to do, and to have the good you desire.

The Law of Mind works in all areas of your life — health, happiness, love, success, prosperity, and money. There is no reason for anyone in the world (and *you* especially!) to experience a shortage in any of these areas.

THINGS TO THINK ON

Answer the following questions to yourself in writing. Get all the blank paper you need and keep writing until you have listed ALL the good you want. Don't you be stingy. God is not stingy.

What do you want to be?
What do you want to do?
What do you want to have?

Remember: You must know where you are going in order to get there.

QUOTES TO REMEMBER

"A journey of a thousand miles begins with the first step."   ~ Lao Tzu, 6th Century B.C.

"To thine own self be true. And it shall follow, as the night the day, Thou canst not then be false to any man."   ~ William Shakespeare

"Know thyself."   ~ Plutarch

AFFIRMATIVE TREATMENT

Right here, right now I choose the best idea for myself.

I know that as I build a high idea of myself that I will draw to me all that I can conceive.

And I conceive of new and exciting things for me to be, to do, and to have.

Thank you, Father!

Thank you, God-in-me!

REVIEW QUESTIONS

1. What is self-discovery?

2. What is the true identity of man?

3. Discuss the meaning and purpose of Mind Science.

4. Why is self-image so important?

Chapter 51

THE TRUTH ABOUT YOU
For Christmas

Dr. Frederick Eikerenkoetter

And the angel said unto them, Fear not; for, behold, I bring you good tidings of great joy, which shall be to all people. For unto you is born this day in the city of David a Savior, who is Christ the Lord. Luke 2:10, 11

Know ye not yourselves how Jesus Christ is in you? 2 Corinthians 13:5

A SCIENCE OF LIVING PRINCIPLE

The truth of Jesus is the truth of you and the truth of me.

To some people, Jesus Christ was God's only Son who lived two thousand years ago and is going to come again. But my ideas about Jesus are different. That's why it interested me the other day when a group of youths walked up to me on the street and handed me a religious leaflet. One of them said to me, "Jesus Christ is coming back soon, are you ready to meet Him?"

You know what I said to him, "Now wait just one minute! In the first place, I'm not serving any God that goes and comes. This God that you're talking about that goes and comes and absents Himself from the earth, I'm not concerned with Him." When I said that, their eyes popped and their mouths dropped wide open. They didn't expect that! I told them, "The God that I serve is spoken of in the hymn that says, 'He walks with me, He talks with me, and He tells me that I am His own!'"

The Christ "comes again" when a man remembers who he is in God and who God is in him.

I'm here to tell you that Christ is not just a man or just God's only Son who was here two thousand years ago and went away! Christ is not a dead man on a cross! Christ does not live in the altar of a church! In this Ministry, we teach that **Christ is the Presence of God-in-me and the Presence of God-in-you, now and forever! Christ is the ever-living Presence of God-in-man.**

Now many people hear me preach this and they say to me, "What about the Bible passage which says, *'God so loved the world, that He gave His only begotten Son, that whosoever believeth in Him should not perish, but have everlasting life'*?" (John 3:16) And I explain it to them in this way:

The only begotten Son of God refers to the one Divine Sonship of mankind. Divine Sonship is not exclusive to the person Jesus, but it is inclusive to each individual in the whole world! God so loved mankind that He gave all mankind Divine Sonship. You see Jesus never claimed to be God's only relative. The theologians gave us that idea. You have to be careful of what the theologians tell you.

God so loved all of mankind, that He gave every man Divine Sonship.

Jesus perfectly demonstrated the Christ, the Divinity within. Jesus recognized the truth of His own Divinity. He knew the truth about Himself: He knew who He was in God and who God was in Him. And He knew that He could use the Power of God within to work wonders.

But it is not enough for Jesus to be the ONLY one to realize and demonstrate the Presence of God within. **It is the possibility and the responsibility of every man to come to the same realization**

and demonstration of his own Divinity as Jesus did. Each man must come to know the truth of his own Divine Sonship. And until you know this, you don't know the truth of Jesus.

Each person must come to that inner realization that "I AM WHAT JESUS IS." And you can't know Jesus until you know that you are exactly what Jesus is — the Son of God. The truth of Jesus is the truth of you and the truth of me.

Jesus realized who He was in God, and who God was in Him. And whenever Jesus said, "I and my Father are one," He spoke that truth for every man and of every man. He demonstrated the Presence of God within Him, by healing, by blessing, and by showing love to the whole world. He pointed us to our own Divinity, when He said, *"The works that I do shall you do also."* (John 14:12)

QUOTES TO REMEMBER

"When God individualized Himself in you, He gave you everything you need — the power to accomplish the good you desire."

~ Rev Ike

"According to your faith, so be it unto you."

~ Matthew 9:29

"The Healthy, Happy, Loving, Successful, and Prosperous Presence of God is within you — within me — within everyone."

~ Rev. Ike

"Let each man think himself an act of God, his mind a thought, his life a breath of God; and let each try, by great thoughts and good deeds, to show the most of Heaven he hath in him."

~ Philip James Bailey

AFFIRMATIVE TREATMENT

Right here and right now

I accept the Christ Presence in me.

I accept the God Presence in me.

I accept the God Power in me.

I go forth into life to let this God Presence and God Power flow out of me as health, happiness, love, success, and prosperity.

I AM the perfect realization and demonstration of the Love and Joy of the Lord.

Thank you, Father!

REVIEW QUESTIONS

1. What was the truth of Jesus? How can you best demonstrate this truth?

2. What did Jesus know that many people don't know?

3. How many children does God have?

4. What are the different religious beliefs about Jesus?

A THOUGHT

If you think you are beaten you are.
If you think you dare not you don't.

If you'd like to win but think you can't
it's almost a cinch you won't.

Life's battles don't always go to the
stronger or faster person —

But sooner or later the person who wins
is the one who thinks he can.

Chapter 52

NOW IS THE TIME
For the New Year

Dr. Frederick Eikerenkoetter

Be ye transformed by the renewing of your mind. Romans 12:2

A SCIENCE OF LIVING PRINCIPLE

Now is the only time there is. Yesterday is gone and tomorrow never comes.

Many people wait until the New Year begins to make resolutions about what they want to be, to do, and to have. But in this Ministry we teach you NOT to wait for a certain day or time of the year to change your conditions. We teach you NOT to wait for somebody else or something else to give you the good that you desire. We teach that NOW is the only time there is — the time to change your conditions for the better is <u>right here</u> and <u>right now</u>!

This is a now Ministry. And I'm a <u>now</u> teacher And I'm telling you, through the Presence and Power of God-in-you, you CAN renew your way of life right here and right now! You can change anything in your experience. You can change your life by changing your mind!

Do You Have A "Someday" Attitude?

Many people don't want to change their thinking, and they don't want to change their minds. People want to change everyone and everything but themselves. But if you are waiting for someone else or something else to bring success and prosperity to you, you will never succeed and prosper. If you are waiting for "someday" to overcome your conditions, you're going to be waiting for a long, long time. Because when is "someday"? I've heard of Monday, Tuesday, Wednesday, Thursday, Friday, Saturday, and Sunday, but I've never heard of a day called "someday"!

If you don't have the good you want to have, it's because of your "someday" attitude. Your "someday" attitude is the reason you haven't prospered as you would like to prosper. You see, the ideas in your mind are what cause you to succeed or fail, have prosperity or poverty, to have or not have that which you want.

You are never going to get any further in life than the ideas you have about yourself in your mind.

The Bible says, "Be ye transformed by the renewing of your mind." Now what does that mean? If you are experiencing limitation and you want to experience abundance, you must change your mind about yourself. You must reject the idea in the world-mind that limitation and lack are FACTS of life. Limitation and lack are not the facts of MY life. And they don't have to be the facts of your life. If they are — you have originated them, you have caused them by the thoughts in your own mind. When you change your mind about yourself from one who is limited to one who is blessed with abundance, you will replace limitation with abundance, you will replace lack with plenty.

The Power Is Within You!

If you have the negative belief that you do not have the power within you to experience the health, happiness, love, success, and prosperity you desire, you must change that belief and get an expanded idea of yourself. You must come to know that you CAN have the good that you want through the Presence and Power of God-in-you. Through this Presence of God-in-you, you already have the power to change your conditions and to better your life.

When you know the Presence of God-in-you, your thinking will change from the negative to the positive. Your life will change and you will experience the good you desire — not tomorrow, not next year, not "someday," but <u>right here</u> and <u>right now</u>! You will see that you don't have to wait for somebody else or something else or sometime else to overcome your conditions.

Make Every Day a New Beginning

As you go through the New Year, make it an everyday, continual practice to examine your own thinking. Remember: the Bible says, "As a man thinks, so is he." (Proverbs 23:7) If you are experiencing limitation of some kind or you are not prospering as you would like, examine the thoughts that you think in your mind. Greet each and every day with the attitude that today is the day some good is going to happen to you. Greet each and every day as a new opportunity to magnify and glorify the Presence and Power of God within you. By believing in yourself positively and correctly, you can make every day of the year a good day — a day filled with Health, Happiness, Love, Success, and Prosperity. Through the Presence and Power of God-in-you, you can make every day a new beginning toward a more prosperous, more dynamic, more joyful way of life.

QUOTES TO REMEMBER

"Dost thou love Life? Then do not squander Time; for that's the stuff Life is made of."   ~ Benjamin Franklin

"Don't wait for pie in the sky by-and-by when you die. Get your pie now with ice cream on top!"   ~ Rev. Ike

"The time to change your conditions for the better is <u>right here</u> and <u>right now</u>!"   ~ Rev. Ike

AFFIRMATIVE TREATMENT

Through the Presence and Power of God-in-me, I CAN change all my conditions and live a happy, healthy, more successful and prosperous life.

I AM experiencing the good I desire right here and right now!

Thank you, God-in-me, my Infinite Source of All Good.

REVIEW QUESTIONS

1. What is it that you want most out of life? Have you achieved it? If not, what is keeping you from that good?

2. How do you view each new day? What should your attitude be? Why?

3. How can you change your life?

4. Should you wait until the New Year begins to make positive changes in your life? Why or why not?

5. Are you succeeding and prospering as you would like? If not, what should you do?

God will meet you at the point of your need.

Here are some little prayers which I have given literally millions of people. These little prayers have brought big answers, big "miracles," big solutions. Pray these with feeling and faith. They will bring you:

"THE ANSWER THAT YOU NEED!"

The Problem-Solving Prayer/The Answer-Bringing Prayer
When you need an answer or need a problem solved: open your mind to the answer that you need. Believe that God has the very answer, the very solution to your problem. *"Let go and let God have His wonderful way!" "His ways are past finding out."* (Romans 11:33) Mentally turn loose the problem, open your mind to God and pray in your heart:

> God-in-me is my answer, right now. And the answer is happening right now. I see it. I feel it in my heart. Thank you, God-in-me.

The Prayer That Prevents and Cures Worry

> God-in-me is my everything, and I don't have to worry about anything. Thank you, God-in-me.

Prayer for Your Healing and Continued Good Health

> God-in-me is my healing and my good health, right now. I see it. I feel it in my heart. Thank you, God-in-me.

Prayer for Healing and Continued Good Health of Loved Ones, Friends, or Any Other Person
Think of the ones for whom you wish to pray and mentally see and feel them being healed and kept in good health. Call the person's name and say this prayer:

> (Name), God-in-you is your healing and good health, right now. I see it. I feel it in my heart. Thank you, God-in-me.

Prayer for Happiness, Love, and Friendship

God-in-me guides me into ways of happiness, love and friendship. Knowing that God is in me makes me happy. The presence of God-in-me makes me a powerful person. I have the power of happiness. I have the power of love. I have the power of friendship. And I now let my God-Given Power of happiness, love and friendship fill my life with happiness, love and all of the right people for every right purpose. I give and receive happiness, love and friendship in Divine Order. Thank you, God-in-me.

Prayer for Success and Prosperity

"In all your ways, acknowledge Him and He will direct your paths." (Proverbs 3:6)

I now recognize God-in-me as my guide and power of success and prosperity. I see and feel God-in-me guiding me from success to success, from prosperity to prosperity. I desire only that which is good for myself and everyone. My success and prosperity glorify God and uplift all mankind. In my mind, I see God-in-me making me an example and inspiration of success and prosperity to encourage others. Thank you, God-in-me, for success and prosperity.

Prayer for Money

I now recognize God-in-me as my Source and Supply of all Good, including money. I believe that God wants me to have surplus Good, including surplus money. Money to meet my needs. Money to pay my bills. Money to enjoy. I open my mind to money. I desire money only for good purposes. I will think right about money. I will do right about money. I will give right about money. I do not serve money. Money serves me. I see and feel never-ending streams of money pouring into my life for every good purpose. I love it and enjoy it. Thank you, God-in-me, for money and all Good.

Printed in Great Britain
by Amazon